"Here we have essays that have passed through a shrinking machine, stories thick as bread, poems clean as mirrors; here we have Holy Mother facing off against All Saints; here kestrels and shrews and a hawk giving a ground squirrel a make-over; here we have diapers and dictators; here a missive from Lazarus; here elegies and jeremiads; here St. Francis meets Mel Brooks; here we have the Dalai Lama playing Name that Tune; here a concatenation of questions about the soul; here we have what I would do if I were pope; here free throws as worship, holding hands as prayer; here we have Brother Brian Doyling up the world for us yet again, awe and aha, as no one else can."

—Lance Larsen, poet laureate of Utah

A Shimmer of Something

Lean Stories of Spiritual Substance

Brian Doyle

Foreword by

Jill Peláez Baumgaertner

LITURGICAL PRESS

Collegeville, Minnesota

www.litpress.org

Cover design by Stefan Killen Design. Cover photo by Joseph Doyle.

The quotation in "What Joseph Mitchell Might Have Been Doing in His Office at The New Yorker in Those Last Thirty Years during Which He Did Not Publish" is adapted from Roger Angell, Postscript, "Joseph Mitchell," *The New Yorker* (June 10, 1996): 80.

Library of Congress Cataloging-in-Publication Data

Doyle, Brian, 1956 November 6–
    A shimmer of something : lean stories of spiritual substance / Brian Doyle.
        pages   cm
    ISBN 978-0-8146-3714-2 — ISBN 978-0-8146-3739-5 (e-book)
    1. Spirituality—Meditations.   I. Title.

  BL624.2.D69   2014
  242—dc23   2013042280

For my brother Peter Joseph Doyle,
with love and admiration

How I would love to speak
To everybody on the street
Just for once to break the rules
I know it would be so cool

—Joe Strummer, "Willesden to Cricklewood"

Poetry is "memorable speech . . . about birth, death, the Beatific Vision . . . the awards and miseries of desire, the unjust walking the earth and the just scratching miserably for food like hens, triumphs, earthquakes, deserts . . . the gratifications and terrors of childhood, the impact of nature . . . the despairs and wisdoms of the mature . . . the mark on the wall, the joke at luncheon, word games . . . the dance of a stoat . . . the raven's gamble . . . "

—W. H. Auden, *The Poet's Tongue*

Contents

Foreword

I have always called them "box poems," each poem a rectangle of words that somehow, always, ends up perfect on the page with justified margins and nothing leftover. Take the lid off and you will see, crammed corner to corner, characters ardently living and fiercely dying; children vastly loved by the parents they frustrate; good priests and bad; the exhilaration of the game, usually basketball but sometimes baseball; and all of the sad, thrilling, reverent, heartrending events of a life copiously lived.

The poet calls them "proems," perhaps part prose, part poem or, even better, part prayer, part poem; and they are that, too. The traditional appellation "prose poem" also fits but in the end does not do them justice, for they offer more than any prose poem I have ever read. Whatever this odd and original genre is, it is irresistible, and my file of accepted poems at *The Christian Century* is bulging with them. Like an addict, I can never get enough, and now, it seems, I am also something of a hoarder with Brian Doyle poems, accepted but not yet typeset, piling up for future savoring by eager readers. I now regularly receive weak imitations of these box poems from other poets who have seen what Brian Doyle does and are now trying it out for themselves. Feeble attempts, of course, reminders that no one but Doyle can write a Doyle proem.

At the heart of what drives these poems is story. "Or here's a story," the poet begins several poems, or "Every day, as you know, one story arrives / And bangs on your head like it was a door." And the stories are everywhere, ready to be coaxed out of a person Doyle meets, or rediscovered in childhood memories, or imagined as he walks through a cemetery full of "stories buried." Stories, he insists, are "so often how we say the things we do not say." Brian Doyle is, above all, a storyteller, his own story and those he tells of others connecting in a long line back to another Storyteller, who used parables to say to his listeners, "Pay attention!"

And that is what these box poems do best: entice us into paying attention. As Doyle writes,

You know how everything seems normal and usual and orthodox
But actually everything if you look at it closely with all four eyes
Is utterly confusing and puzzling and mysterious and astonishing?

We live our lives in a daze, and how much of what surrounds us do we ever really see, or for that matter how much of what happens to us do we ever really remember? "Sometimes we are starving to see every bit of what is right in front of us," Doyle writes. It is not just that we miss the facts of our lives as they whiz by us on their way to the deep recesses of our un-memory. It is that we miss the true nature of reality—that which happens to us every day of our lives—which contains mystery, and if we miss that, we miss the reason for our existence.

So, yes, these poems are in part prayers. I usually intensely resist this identification of poetry with prayer because prayers, in spite of all of the words we may use to craft them or to cry them or to fervently and silently mouth them, are so often either too carefully planned, too rote, or, alternatively, too deep for words. That, too, Brian Doyle knows, and he reaches into the box and pulls out yet another story that once again surprises us, steering us away from the predictable and routine, saying all of those things that are unsayable, and capturing our attention so that we can see what we were just about to miss.

Jill Peláez Baumgaertner

Acknowledgments

Many of these tiny inky lads and lasses appeared in magazines and newspapers and webzines and such, which was a great pleasure (for me, anyway), and I bet they made readers around the world spit out their coffee and call the cops. *Boy*, it's fun to have a proem in print. My particular thanks to Jill Peláez Baumgaertner of *The Christian Century*, Cathy O'Connell-Cahill of *U.S. Catholic*, Paul Lake of *First Things*, Jim Torrens, SJ, of *America*, Philip Harvey of *Eureka Street* in Australia, and Tim McKee, Andrew Snee, and Sy Safransky of *The Sun*, in North Carolina, for their constant crazy generosity.

Many thanks also to Kim Rogers at *Kauai Backstory*, Langdon Hammer at *The American Scholar*, Don Miller at *Notes from the Dells* (the cheerful newsletter of the cool Severson Dells Nature Center in Rockford, Illinois), Michael Pollak of *The New York Times*, Steve Charles at *Wabash College Magazine*, Ed Paladino at *The Wine Explorer*, Marc Covert and John Richen of the excellent e-zine *Smokebox*, the effervescent and gentle Bruno Lettieri at *Platform Magazine* at Victoria University in Australia, Ben George at *Ecotone*, Douglas Burton-Christie at *Spiritus*, Nancy Cook at *Rain Magazine* at Clatsop Community College in Oregon, Greg Wolfe and Mary Kenagy Mitchell at *Image*, Jay Bates at *A River & Sound Review*, and Patrick Madden at *Inscape* (edited by writing students at the estimable Brigham Young University in Utah).

Brian Doyle

A Quiet Sergeant Tells a Story

A plane crashes into a building and people jump
Out of the windows and he catches, in this order,
A small man, a small woman, a tiny shy woman,
A small woman, and finally an *imposing* woman,
As he says. She pause a second before she jump,
He says, and she yells down to me *I am real fat!*
And I yell you jump *now!* which made her jump,
And I bend my knees, you know, to try to reduce
The blow but my back has been all a mess since.
We been friends since then, six years to the day.
We laugh a little now at how we met each other.
She says honey no man but my husband put his
Hands there before or since, and then she laugh.
One hundred eighty-nine people were murdered
That day at the Pentagon where she worked, but
Not her, so she says her job is to remember them
And not let their memory be murdered too, crazy
The good Lord let the fattest lady in the building
Be the one to make it, price being one sergeant,
His poor back, and God bless me if she and I do
Not laugh and laugh when she says that, though
I have to tell you, it hurts like the devil to laugh.

Lines on Discovering a Vast City of Thirteen-Lined Ground Squirrels While Shuffling in Calvary Cemetery on a Brilliant Afternoon Deep in Illinois

Where you wouldn't *believe* the endless armies of corn eight feet tall
And seas of whispering soybeans, and hawks every other phone pole,
And clouds the size of aircraft carriers, and apparently seven million
Ground squirrels about ten inches long and quick and lean as arrows,
Who do indeed have thirteen gold lines in their russet deerskin coats
As I discover while bellied by a burrow and one pops up and sees me
And nearly has a heart attack on the spot, he sort of moans and faints
And slumps back in the hole like some kind of furry Blanche DuBois,
And it hurts my feelings to be seen as such a horror and terror and all
And I scrinch up closer to the hole and speak into it and say *hey man,*
Don't be such a drama queen, I am not here to eat you, and by god if
A *second* thirteen-lined ground squirrel doesn't pop up, a redder one,
And we are about three inches apart, and while the craven part of me
Immediately thinks I might be about to have my roomy nose reduced,
The rest of me is so startled that as usual I start rambling all freeform,
So there I am at age fifty on my belly in the grass amid vast cornfields
Telling a squirrel that yes, it's interesting that this cemetery is divvied
Up into Saints Michael, Maximilian, Martin, Joseph, Clare, & Thérèse,
And it's haunting to find all these young soldiers, and girls married age
Seventeen and eighteen and all, and whole entire clans buried together,
And there's something incredibly moving to me in cemeteries, all those
Stories buried there really, all those riveting hours of all those lives, all
The adventure and misadventure and grace and pain and joys and wars,
But what really nailed me this afternoon was the lengthy line of graves

To the west, along Falconer Road, those are all the babies who died at
A day or a week or a month or a year old, some of their stones grassed
Over so that you had to kneel down and clear it away to see the names.
I don't know, I said to the squirrel, it just seemed the right thing to do
To clear away the grass a little. Maybe that's a kind of creaky prayer.
All this time the squirrel was staring at me with that wild blank regard
That animals have, you know, like they are from a galaxy far far away,
And the instant that I stopped speaking, having nothing further to say,
He or she disappeared utterly, and I staggered up and shuffled back to
Saint Joseph's block, feeling that he above all men would understand.

The Black Dog

Driving through a dense dark moist night by the ocean
I ask my friend *hey man how you doing* and he is quiet
A few minutes because he knows I mean the black dog
And he wants to answer the unanswerable without lies,
Without the usual bob and weave and dodge and parry.

The tide isn't all the way out, he says. I trip on the dog.
I carry a piece of paper in my wallet with all the names
Of all the things I love. It's a really long list. The other
Day I got it laminated because it was getting all messy.
People must think I'm some kind of religious crackpot

Or lost and checking directions because I pull it out all
The time. But I sure need to read *that* map, you know?
There's a long silence in the car after that and then out
In the ocean there's an incredible moaning bellow, real
Loud and long, it must be a tanker or a barge or a ferry

Or something, and we totally lose it laughing, and then
Spend some minutes speculating that it's a blue whale
Passing a kidney stone or a lighthouse with major lust,
After which we spend the rest of the trip telling stories,
Which is so often how we say the things we do not say.

On Pinning the Number 92 on My Son before Basketball Tryouts

His back all tense and a dagger of sweat down the middle of his shirt like a blade.
I try to cut the heat by saying man, ninety-two, what are you, a defensive tackle?
But he's not exactly in the mood which I can tell just from the tone of his silence.
I fumble with the safety pins to make sure all four corners are tacked down tight.
The last thing you need at tryouts is your number flapping in the wind like a geek.
I get three pins in clean and fiddle around the last one a while on purpose because
I am utterly overwhelmed and am trying not to kneel down in the echoing hallway
And cry and bang my head on the icy concrete because I love this boy more than I
Can ever tell you or explain even to myself and I *so* want him to do well and make
The team but he might not and then I would have to give him the speech about how
To mill pain into accomplishment, how to turn it on the lathe of your will and such,
You know the speech, you got it from your dad, I got it from mine, every dad ever
Has to give that speech eventually which stinks because it means every child ever
Sooner or later feels the hot lick of disappointment and pain and embarrassment &
Humiliation, the girl says no, your name's not on the roster posted on the gym wall,
You punt the test, you miss the shot, and this is not even to mention the major pain
That comes for us all but in the best of worlds comes later in life and not when you
Are a kid like this boy with my hand on his shoulder in the roiling hall by the gym.
I click the last pin and cup his face in my hand and say dude, I love you, be *quick*,
Be *yourself*, be *relentless*, and we touch fists and he runs off with the other players
And I stand there shaking so bad one of the other dads looks at me apprehensively
Like is he going to have to phone the emergency medical techs or what so I shuffle
Outside into the wild wet air and try not to think about anything at all whatsoever
But as usual I wonder why the very best thing is the one thing that hurts the worst.

On Trying to Explain a Friend's Divorce
to My Young Son in the Kitchen One Morning

Why? he says, while working away at a tiny piece of toast and a vast mountain of jam.
They just weren't getting along, is probably the best way to explain it, I guess, I mutter,
And then for the next few minutes as I perform the coffee ablutions and he guzzles jam
And neither of us says a word I think of all the words that could be said but will not be,
Affair and recrimination and despair and arguments and shrieking and weeping and lies,
And kids and counselor and house and pain and contract and money and rights and law,
And visitation and separation and tears and grief and disbursement and death of warmth,
And all the other words now packed in boxes, joy and babies and laughter and promises,
All the hard work between them, all those dishes washed, all those nights with sick kids,
All those days side by side silent in the garden and one handing the other a bottle of beer
Without a word and the other grins and they sit for a moment watching hawks overhead,
All the conversational lines they finished for each other at dinners with friends, all those
Hours driving when nothing needed to be said because each knew the other well enough
So that one would turn the radio louder just when she sensed he was weary at the wheel,
All the times he did what he did not want to do because he knew it would mean so much,
All the mornings when neither was awake but neither was asleep and the hours were rife
With small pains and great promise, when no matter what broke they would figure it out.
They just weren't getting along is probably the best way to explain it, I say again quietly,
And my son, a subtle and intelligent man, finishes mowing the mountain and disappears.

Ball

Long ago I dated a woman who turned out to be even more unbalanced than me.
This is a most remarkable statement because I was a parade of idiots at the time.
Our affair soured almost immediately but neither of us had the guts to surrender.
Finally one night we had a screaming roaring shrieking fight and I snarled *I quit.*
She said *If you break up with me I will kill myself and have you beaten to death.*
She said this very cold and calm and indeed she knew lots of thugs and convicts.
I knew her well enough by then to know she was completely and utterly serious.
Any intelligent man would at this point have approached police and/or attorneys
And moved abroad and changed his name and face and filed off his fingerprints,
But I drove home, at about two in the morning, and got into my basketball stuff,
And dribbled down the street to the park and shot baskets until the sun came up.
I remember shooting and shooting until I was sure my arm was going to fall off.
The streetlights clicked off as I walked real slow back to my ratty old apartment.
This sounds like a totally stupid male way to deal with a crisis but everyone has
Places they go when they are scared and exhausted and have to just go mindless.
The same thing happened when my grandma was dying when I was age twelve,
We would go to see her in her clean white quiet room where she got tinier each
Day and when we would get home my sweet mama would say *is there anything
You want to talk about* but I would already be down the street with my holy ball
And at the park I would run past all the games and all the guys waiting for nexts
And find an empty court and just shoot and shoot. It's sort of hard to find words
For what it meant to me, and the ball is so far gone from my hungry hands now
That it seems crazy to even try to articulate it. You will think I'm melodramatic
When I say maybe basketball saved my life, but I leave you with this one image:
A guy in the middle of the night in a city long ago with his hands shaking so bad
He could hardly get a grip on the ball, but an hour later, under the old streetlight,
I hit like eleven in a row and was panting and pleased and something was healed.

Herself

Not a day passes when I do not feel the presence of Our Lady,
The old priest says. Not a day. I was thirteen when she spoke.
A headlong colt loose in the hills and forests of the Dakotas.
You would think epiphany would come in the wilderness but
Not to me. I heard Her voice as I waited in the butcher's shop.
Unmistakable and clear as the day is short where I was raised.
Fled Her down the nights and down the days, as the poet says,
But there came a moment when I knew I could flee no longer,
At which point I took train to the seminary and found my call
Down the arches of the years and down the labyrinthine ways.
That's your man Francis Thompson, as loony as a jaybird, yet
Utterly correct about how we run away from our deepest soul.
Anyway we were talking about the daily presence of Herself.
There's no set time and there's no illumination or aura or that
Sort of hokey stuff, just Her voice speaking clearly in my ear.
A melodious voice, you might say, and speaking English, yes.
As to what She is talking about I think that is a private matter,
You understand. But I am not getting all pious. She's amused
Sometimes and sometimes there's a sort of thrill in Her voice.
We forget She was once a shy Jewish woman in a dry village.
I should conclude by telling you one odd thing. When young
I tried to write down what She said but very soon discovered
It could not be done and quite literally no words would come.
What She has to say is for your ear and your heart alone, yes?

In Memory of the Ten Thousand Basiji

In the beginning of the war the mullahs sent animals into the minefields,
Beginning with dogs but then proceeding to donkeys, horses, and mules.
This tactic however proved fruitless, as when one died all fled headlong,
So the decision was made to use boys from ages twelve through sixteen.
Soon it was ordered that each boy enter the minefield wrapped in a robe,
So that parts of bodies from the explosions did not litter the field of fire.
The chief of the mullahs imported thousands of plastic keys from Taiwan.
Each boy was given a key to paradise before he walked into the minefield.
When the war ended after eight years some ten thousand boys were dead.
You can still find keys here and there if you are looking very attentively.
You can still find some of the men who sent those boys into the minefields.
One of them is now the president of the country where the boys blew up.
Every time he opens his mouth and says something defiant and murderous
I hear a mine explode and see a key whirling through the air like a dagger.
Every time he opens his mouth and says anything at all I want to hand him
A key and wrap him in a white robe and set him walking out into the fields.

Poem for Those Who Are About to Wed

As for advice, I don't have any advice for you,
And anyone who says they have advice for you,
My advice is to run away screaming and roaring,
But hold hands as you run, and if one of you gets
A bit ahead of the other he or she should hold out
His or her hand for the other, and he or she fading
Should stick out a hand & say quiet *yo, little help?*
This doesn't count as advice because as you know
I have no advice about anything whatsoever at all,
But you'd be surprised how saying *yo, little help?*
Actually leads to a little help, and the ball returns,
And the game bursts out all complex and brilliant
And mysterious and extraordinary and miraculous
Again, but in new ways you never even imagined.
A total mystery, and maybe the coolest thing ever.
Best of luck. Keep me posted. Accept *no* advice.

Things I Am No Good At (Selection)

Girls, carpentry, patience, hunting, plumbing, writing plays.
Appreciating ballet, mime, and performance art of all kinds.
Arriving at anything like cordial terms with rap and hiphop.
Giving anyone on any talk radio station the slightest chance.
Flying a plane, filling out tax forms, letting laundry stack up.
Meetings. Writing that is far more catharsis than connection.
Confession done with a wink as a form of lucrative theatrics.
Peering beneath the surface of shrill insistence on legitimacy.
Hiking, biking, milking, bilking, dancing, prancing, courting.
Singing, although I must note that I am an excellent hummer,
Persistent and relentless to the point of driving people insane.
My kids for example laugh at me and then after a while tartly
Say *dad* in the way they say *dad* when what they really mean
Is *daaaaad your off-key moaning droning is embarrassing us*.
The thought occurs to me, in what I hope is the middle of my
Remarkable existence, that the one thing I am totally good at
Is mortifying my kids, which doesn't seem an altogether bad
Thing to be good at. I mean, first they laugh, which is a good
Thing, and then even as they roll their eyes all drama queeny
For their friends, they are sort of grinning, not at all ashamed
Of the old man, that's just what he's *like*, their dad, not at all
Like the other dads who can fix cars and invest mutual funds.
In fact the fact of the matter is that whenever I get pretty dark
About mutual funds and crisis planning and the creaky house,
I find myself humming, or more accurately I am *told* that I'm
Humming by an exasperated child, but the half-grin he wears
When he says that, or the smile *she* wears—that's everything.

The Second Letter of Lazarus to His Sisters

Beloveds, I don't think we are quite communicating clearly here.
What I *said* was that I think there are two sides to every miracle,
And while I am *thrilled* to be alive, & not moldering in the grave,
And I have written any number of letters of gratitude to Himself,
It *was* inarguably embarrassing to be stripped of the graveclothes
With which I was bound hand and foot, and to stand there stark
Naked, discombobulated after being called forth by a loud voice,
Nor was my skin in what you all would call the pink of condition,
Nor had I eaten in four days, but there I was suddenly on display.
You would be rattled too, you know you would, the both of you.
Loose him and let him go, He says, and everyone ooos and aaas,
But, you know, then what? You remember what happened next,
He moves away down the hill and everyone follows, the fastest
Sprinting to the front to see what will happen next, the vendors
Packing their foods and wares to move along to the next miracle,
But there I am naked as a jaybird and smelling to high heaven,
Famished, stunned, reborn, in debt, confused, and utterly alone.
I cast no aspersions when I remark that you both followed Him.
I would have too, had I been capable, and now that I am healthy
I will follow him to the second end of my days. But do allow me
Simply to note that while it surely was the most *memorable* day
Of my entire life, it also certainly was not the most comfortable,
Or the easiest, or even, dare I say, the best. To me the day I was
Married was the best day, or the days my three children arrived.
So I can say, even as I am the most thankful man who ever was,
That I regret, in some small way, that for many centuries hence
I will be not Eleazar, a decent man, beloved of his many friends,

A good father, a patient husband, noted for his kindness and wit,
But only Lazarus who was by the Christ returned from the dead.
If such be the small price of this new life in which I am at home
Again in the arms of those I love, among whom I count you two,
So be it; but I do think that you, among all women in the world,
Would understand that miracles breed ripples that do not cease.

At Mount Saint Joseph's Home

Friend of mine died yesterday morning, just before lunch.
He was old and frail and hadn't really eaten at all in years,
So it wasn't a surprise, and he was waaay deep in the past
In his head these last days, they say, talking to his parents,
So it wasn't like he was going to make a roaring comeback
Or anything, it's best for him to go, to rest, to see his folks,
To actually sit down and savor a thorough dinner for once,
But still, you know, now he won't come in and plop down
And beam at me, and primly zip open his ancient briefcase,
And start in fidgeting about this or that or nine other things,
And when someone dies, someone you sure liked although
He drove you raving muttering moaning gibbering insane,
You sit for a moment and try to remember the last minute
You had with him, because it's a real momentous minute,
And in my case he was in a ghastly echoing hospice room,
And it was incredibly hot, he had a moist cloth on his face,
And he had on a beautiful pressed dress shirt but no pants,
Just his boxers, and checkered boxers too, God help us all,
And those tiny white socks that girls and ill old men wear,
And the scene was so awkward I had to cut it with a joke,
You know how you issue a dry remark and hide behind it,
So I said, *Art, this is really weird to see you sans trousers,*
And there's a long pause, the machines beeping, a scream
Somewhere far away, cars whizzing by like wasps outside,
And then faint but clear as a bell comes my friend's voice:
But, ah, it's a really lovely pressed shirt, don't you think?

14

Crash

There was a moment after the horrific car crash that I wish to tell you about.
It wasn't the crash itself, which occurred because of the usual greed for time,
Because a guy jumped out when he shouldn't have and then there was blood,
And it wasn't the long moments after when things slowly kept on happening,
A tall calm guy on his cell phone calling the cops, a woman crying in her car,
Smoke drifting, one of the drivers moaning, glass everywhere it shouldn't be,
Soon enough the approaching demanding wail of cop cars and the ambulance,
The first impatient honk of a car stuck a few cars behind where they can't see
What happened or hear the guy moaning or see the woman sobbing in her car,
The first car inching past the broken smoking cars, the driver reluctant but he
Has got to get to work, man, there's nothing he can do, someone called a cop,
No, we know those moments, we have all seen those moments, we have been
In those moments, God help us, and we have each and every one of us driven
Through the shatter and the smoke, past the moaning and weeping and shock,
But there was something about the first minute after the crash that haunts me
To the point where I have to write it down even though I know I am not good
Enough to catch the shiver of it, the tremble, the way everyone within earshot
Stopped whatever momentous or thoughtless or normal thing they were doing
And focused on who among us was hurt, paid the most ferocious attention for
Once not on who we are and what we do, but who *they* are and what *they* did,
Or what was done upon them. I swerved out of the way, shocked and cursing
Like everyone else, but as I sat there rattled and thinking my back was busted
This time for sure, I saw four people jump out of their cars and run like crazy
To where there was pain. All the rest of the day I've smelled shame and hope.

What Joseph Mitchell Might Have Been Doing in His Office at The New Yorker in Those Last Thirty Years during Which He Did Not Publish

Learning Persian, studying the meticulous plumbing of cats,
Studying all the chess matches of José Raúl Capablanca y
Graupera, reading Myles na gCopaleen in the original Irish,
Mapping, by hand, with many colored pencils, the vast web
Of the Long Island Rail Road and its byzantine antecedents,
Trying to write a novel in which the number seven is a hero,
Trying to remember every single word his mother ever said
To him in the moist adventures of his childhood in Carolina,
Tasting every single wine made one year in one small town,
Writing down every smell he ever smelled in his whole life,
If possible in the order smelled, starting with the wet chalky
Smell of milk and sweat and hickory trees and the ten cows,
And proceeding up to and including the smell of the pencils
On his desk. Perhaps he carefully considered the trajectories
Of baseballs, the way they sail off bats at every conceivable
Angle, or perhaps he considered the miracles of mammalian
Bats, from the bumblebee bat which weighs less than a dime
To the flying fox, which has a wingspan of say, Joe Mitchell.
"Each morning," said a friend, "he would step off the elevator
With a preoccupied air, nod wordlessly, and close himself in
His office. He emerged at lunchtime, always wearing his hat,
And after being gone ninety minutes, he would again vanish
Into his office, closing the door. Not much typing was heard
From within, and people who called on Joe reported that his
Desktop was empty of everything but paper and pencils. On

The elevator down at the end of the day he would sometimes
Emit a small sigh but he never complained, never explained."
Yet it seems to me that the mystery of what Joe Mitchell did
In those last thirty years during which he published no essay
Is the other way around; it's what he *did* do, not what he did
Not do, that's sweet and piercing, and I bet a buck that what
He did do when he wasn't typing was even more remarkable
Than what he had done. In fact I think this is true of all of us.
I think maybe he was one of the greatest listeners of all time,
Myself, and that's what I admire the guy for, not the ink trail
He left behind until he stopped typing. Perhaps it was spring,
Early in the afternoon, one of those startling hot spring days,
And his office window was open, and a bee droned, and way
Down the street a kid hammered a baseball, and that finished
It for Joe Mitchell, he figured if he couldn't write that sound
Down he shouldn't write at all; or maybe he concluded right
Then that recording wasn't as great an art as being a witness.

On College Street,
in Sydney,

I meet a guy with a truly heroic beard, not to mention the cool black robe
And cowl and staff he carries with a worked gold-plated knob on the end,
But it's the beard that gets me, this is a beard like old Walt Whitman and
My boy Herman Melville, a beard with *presence*, a beard that's been at it
For a really long time, years and years, and it is a mark of my lack of tact
That the first words that occur to me leap out of my mouth like tiny trout,
I ask Do you trim that here and there or just let it roam wherever it grows,
And the man with the beard, who turns out to be His Eminence Stylianos,
Archbishop of the Greek Orthodox Church of Australia, loses it laughing
And says You wouldn't believe how many kids ask me that question, it's
Like my beard has a life of its own or something, which I suppose it does
In a sense, I have grown this beard since I was fifteen years old, and soon
He and I are comparing notes on ratty wispy teenage guy scraggle-beards,
And how when you look back on it you can't believe you ever showed up
In public with such a third armpit on the point of your jaw, but that's why
Guys are guys, whether they grow up to be eminent archbishops or dopey
Writers, they do guy things like that, like walk around all sort of roostery,
And have a million collisions with other guys and with walls, and pop out
Words before the words have run through the halting filter of the seething
Brain, and brandish pastoral staffs and hurley sticks and shillelaghs & all,
But just as we get to laughing about the subtle nutty joy of carrying sticks,
His driver drives up and glares ferociously at me and His Eminence has to
Get back to work. We shake hands, the guy has hands the size of racquets,
And off he goes to further the mission of that ancient and bearded Church.
Ever after whenever I read anything his Church, like in the morning news
That one of his brother archbishops died, I remember those few moments,
And how just for a minute, and a rare pause I bet it was, he was just a guy.

At about Noon Pacific Time

A guy twisted on awful drugs drops a baby
From an overpass over a highway in a city,
And a guy driving toward the overpass sees
What's happening and immediately goes for
It, he slams his car into warp drive, he's got
A convertible, he's got an infinitesimal shot
At catching the baby but he can't get to him,
The baby smashes and the guy sheers away,
And like everyone else who sees this he has
To pull over and weep for a real long while.
He doesn't tell anyone about hitting the gas
Except his wife and even that takes a week.
She is merciful and knows him real well so
She asks him about angles and acceleration
And stuff like that and soon he is sketching
Possible angles of capture and how the boy
Could fairly easily have landed safely if he
Was rotating properly and kids are rubbery
Anyways, you'd be surprised how children
Bounce up after unreal crashes and wrecks,
It's the speed of gravity versus acceleration,
How fast he is falling racing how fast I can
Get there, there was a decent chance, but . . .
And she interrupts him real gentle and says
You went for it, that's all I ask of you, ever.

A Note on Sobbing

Yesterday the woman who married me heard a child cry for hours and hours.
You hardly ever hear a child cry for hours and hours, usually it's just a burst,
But this time she said the child, a girl, age thirteen, sobbed up her whole soul
Right there in the hospital ward for hours, her poor mom sitting there silently.
Finally the girl stopped crying, I guess she had nothing left inside, you know,
But I have been thinking about sobbing since, and how sobbing is not crying,
Or weeping or tearing up, no, sobbing is just like having your guts torn apart,
And you haven't the slightest control, it's not at all like tears, where you can
Finally sort of command yourself to get a grip, to cool down, to shudderingly
Get back to the surface again, or like weeping, which is a crazy thunderstorm
That's intense for a few minutes and then passes, leaving everything dripping.
No, sobbing is *sobbing*, even the sound hints at what's really happening here,
You sob so hard your breath staggers, everything you ever were is utterly lost,
And you sit or kneel or bend over at the knees gasping, you lose track of time,
It's like something huge broke that you didn't even know was so deep inside,
And all the water in the universe has to pour out through your guts before any
Kind of new life gets born, blinking. One time years ago I heard a woman sob
Like that, from the bottom of the bone of her heart, pretty much all night long,
While I stood on the other side of the door losing my cockiness & fingernails,
And I sobbed like that one time too, later, in a small quiet chapel, no one else
Was there, I thought, until after about an hour a quiet priest sat down and said
Nothing whatsoever, for which I am still, six years later, really really grateful.
All he did at last was put his hand on my shoulder and that was what I needed
To go back to the body where I used to be, though a new man lived there now.

She

After my late aunt got her third new hip,
The third in an eventual parade of seven,
I call to razz her about having more hips
Now than she had been originally issued,
& she laughed but then characteristically
Sailed off on a disquisition about prayer
And how it did and didn't work hipwise,
And how the doctors had used the bones
Of a deceased woman in her hip surgery,
And how she conversed with the Mother
About this among various other subjects,
And the Mother, noted my cheerful aunt,
Was a woman of endless gentle patience,
For I pepper the poor soul with moaning
And complaints all the blessed day long,
Said my cheerful aunt, and She does not
Tell me to stuff it, or hasn't yet, anyway.
All day long I rattle and prattle and chat
And She listens and then finally I'll stop
Talking at which point I finally hear Her.
I think maybe that's the way She speaks
To everyone but everyone doesn't listen
All that well, that's the greatest problem
With men and women, the first example
In this particular crucial regard being me,
You know what I mean? Ah, yes, you do.

On Being Driven Through Elm Trees
to the Doctor Seven Thousand Times

By my mom when I was a kid, this was forty years ago,
Late in the nineteen sixties in seething New York State,
I had all sorts and shapes of allergies and asthmaticism,
And she drove me to the doctor's week after week after
Week after week after week after week after week after
Week, I think about it now and calculate she must have
Driven ten million miles with me slouching and sulking
And staring out the windows at the parades of the elms.
It was always autumn and always raining and the ranks
Of trees leaned over the hissing road, my mom praying
Over the steering wheel, she had a way of being bowed
Over it, intent, and my mom has a gaze like a goshawk.
We sailed through the wet dark afternoons like arrows.
It seems to me that this went on for thousands of years.
We were always cruising through moist brown streets
In one car or another, in one village or another, the elm
Trees bending over the road, their hands like dinosaurs,
And I cannot remember that I was ever kind or friendly,
That I ever asked my mom anything at all about herself,
That I ever thought that she might be weary or terrified,
That it ever occurred to me that she was a human being.
All I remember is the tall wet trees bowing as we drove,
Their muscled bellies, the way they knuckled the roads.
All the things you think you will remember you will not.
I would like to remember my mom's face as she peered
Into the swirl of dank leaves, I would like to remember

The music of her manner, how her hand spun the wheel,
The sound she made in her throat when she was amused,
Any of the words she said to me, even one of the stories.
But all I remember is the trees and the rain and a hissing
Of tires and the way the leaves spun crazily in our wake.

She Does

I sit with my son at the table when he is six years old
And he tells me about what happened at school today
And he says a sentence to me that I never ever forgot.
This girl I liked who I didn't think liked me, she does,
He said, and there was a look on his face that moment
No one could ever explain but you know what I mean.
The words we could use to try to explain it just glance
Off and fall to the floor and slump in jumbles & heaps.
My son and I sat there for a while not saying anything
Whatsoever. Bet a buck you've been at that table also.

On Being Asked to Keep Score
for the Eighth Grade Basketball Game

By the harried referee who has already adjudicated two games this morning
And has three more left to go before he can go home and reconsider his life.
Of course, I say, and make my way through the burbling stands to courtside
Where the keeper of the clock glances at me imperiously, time being crucial
And the calculus of narrative secondary. The referee hands me the holy pen.
One team represents the Holy Mother, the Madonna, She Who Is, our Mary.
The other team, covering its bets, represents All Saints; a moral complexity,
You would think, do All Saints include the Mother or does She rise above?
But I don't get a chance to ask because the game is away!, the Virgin's men
Suitably in blue and the Saints, for reasons that are unclear, draped in green.
Back and forth they fly for two minutes, lots of shots but no scores, my pen
Hovers, but then there's a river of points and rebounds and assists and fouls
And I am scribbling madly trying to write down the game as it zips past me,
I mention this to the timekeeper, this is sort of a crazy literary endeavor, eh?
But she glares at me and I go back to recording the unrecordable, the Saints
Trying to hold off the relentless creativity of the Madonna, ten things going
On at once, I am constantly behind, for example two Saints hammer a Mary
Man and the ref calls the foul on one guy but I record fouls on both of them,
Feeling that at least on one scoresheet for one game history will be accurate,
But by the time I glance back up the ball is floating through the Saint basket
And I missed the shooter, but in the hilarious way of kids the kid who threw
It up from way too far away and accidentally banked it in, the enormous boy
With the orange ponytail and his headband on backwards, is windmilling his
Arms and making airplane noises, and with joy in my heart I score it for him.

Full in the Face

Or here's a story. A man proposes to his girlfriend in a restaurant
And she says yes. There is hubbub and chaos and joy. The waiter,
A good guy, brings the best wine and makes a fuss about the ring.
The couple spend the next ten years together happy with children,
But they've moved to another town and don't get to the restaurant.
After ten years the man is on a trip and he stops in there for lunch.
The waiter, in the way of waiters in good restaurants, is still there.
The man, in the way of men back in rooms where joys were born,
Recognizes the waiter but in the way of men doesn't say anything.
The ritual of the meal proceeds in its quiet sacramental procession,
The water, the bread, the wine, the fish, the shining cloths, a cigar.
But at the end, as the man is signing for the check and rustling his
Jacket pockets for the tip, the waiter sits down suddenly and grins
And says sir, I remember you, I remember the look of exhilaration
And delight on your face, I remember how that lovely girl beamed
Across the table, that was a blessed moment here, we remember it.
May I ask respectfully after the joy and happiness of your family?
It was a little tiny thing, the man says to me later, telling the story,
But the fact that he remembered us and the moment we were born,
Something about it was just incredibly moving to me. A tiny thing,
That a waiter would remember that after many years, but it wasn't
Tiny to me, somehow it was sweet and momentous and wonderful.
There are so many things like that, you know, we say they are tiny
But they are not at all, it's only you don't see them full in the face.

A Corner of the Cloak

You know how everything seems normal and usual and orthodox
But actually everything if you look at it closely with all four eyes
Is utterly confusing and puzzling and mysterious and astonishing?
For example this morning the world presents me a redtailed hawk,
All shoulders and muscle and glower and a bust like Dolly Parton,
And the hawk completes the life cycle of a young ground squirrel,
Spermophilus beecheyi for those of you scoring the game at home,
And carts his or her repast up to a massive oak and carefully peels
The squirrel like a banana, keeping the protein and letting the skin
Fall to the grass below, where a dog, *canis familiaris* for you fans
At home, sniffs curiously and then looks as ecstatic as I have ever,
And I mean *ever*, seen a dog, and they are in general a happy tribe,
But then the young woman roped to the dog, *homo sapiens girlius*
For those of you scoring at home, yanks the leash and barks *drop!*
And the dog with immense reluctance drops the most enticing pelt
He has ever even imagined in the redolent and wondrous universe,
And the girl picks it up and stares at it a moment and then drops it
With a strangled screech or swallowed scream or disgusted moan,
It's hard to explain exactly the nature of her horrified vocal sound,
And off she goes at a canter, dragging the rueful and reluctant dog.
I stand thirty feet away, with my jaw hanging open like a window,
Having witnessed the whole mad sequence from hawk to horrified,
And conclude, for the thousandth time, *what* a wild & blessed gift,
What a bloody and magical machine it is, *what* a slather of stories,
What an endless thicket! You really and truly could be issued fifty
Lifetimes, and spend each of them addled and muddled in wonder,
And never understand or even *see* more than a corner of the cloak.

The Boy Who Only Saw Cranes

A guy in green doctor scrubs tells me a story.
We had a boy here once whose brain locked,
He says, and all he could see or hear or think
About was cranes, sandhill cranes, you know,
The huge birds like herons on major steroids.
Now, fixation or obsession is fairly orthodox,
That's why God made so many psychiatrists,
But this was something totally off the charts,
The poor kid couldn't sleep or function at all.
Essentially he had a mental electric freakout,
Is the easiest way to try to describe the event.
Anyway we tried everything you could think,
Drugs, therapy, psychiatry, prayer, a famous
Football player came by to visit him a while,
His gramma came and did Nez Perce smoke,
Some ancient ceremony like that, but we got
Nowhere, and that kid was starting to vanish
When we finally got the bright idea of going
Out to Sauvie Island and getting a real crane.
Well, you can't bring a bird into the hospital,
Those things are like five feet high and eight
Feet wide, so we take the boy out in my jeep,
And it's the migration season, there they are
Overhead, croaking like anything, and down
They come into the muddy fields like planes.
We stayed there all day with the kid, me and
Two nurses, and whatever it was that needed

To happen in the kid's head, it happened. So
A couple days later he's okay and his family
Comes and gets him and everything ends up
Fine, but here's my question: What was that
All about? So we tell that story here anytime
Someone gets cocky about modern medicine.
Man, I been a doctor for nearly twenty years,
And I tell you there's a new lesson every day,
Sandhill cranes, man, you figure *that* one out!

Woodrow Wilson Startles His Audience with Sudden Prescience about Terrorism while Addressing a Roiling Congress, 1917

I have called this Congress into extraordinary session
Because there are serious choices of policy to be made
Which it is not right nor permissible for me to make alone.
We are here confronted with cruel, unmanly, & ruthless acts
By criminals that throw to the winds all scruples and respect
For the understandings that underlie the intercourse of the world.
They have caused wanton and wholesale destruction of the lives
Of innocent noncombatants, peaceful men, women, and children
For which the doom of retribution must and will come upon them;
The challenge is not only to this sovereign state but to all mankind.
Yet I insist, I abjure, I declare, that we must put heated feeling away.
Our motive will not be revenge or the victorious assertion of might,
But only the vindication of human right of which we are a champion.

There is one choice we cannot make, that we are incapable of making:
We will not choose the path of submission, and suffer the sacred rights
Of our nation and of all people to be ignored or violated; those wrongs
Against which we now array ourselves cut to the very root of human life.
Instead we accept this challenge of hostile purpose because we well know
That in such aggressors we can never have friends; and that in the person
Of powers that smile and chant and offer praise at the murder of children,
We face foes against whom we will spend all our force to check & nullify.
But I say to you this crucial night that we will *not* bring murder to murder.
We will not loose a hail of bullets and bombs upon them and their villages.
We will loose instead the furious weaponry of our capacious intelligence,
The finely honed swords of creativities beyond our enemies' imagination,
For their minds, dimmed by blood, are the very cause of their annihilation;

And we will not destroy them, thereby elevating them to their martyrdom,
But reduce them to that status they so richly deserve, prisoners unto death.

For they are not enemies in a great war of civilizations, as they proclaim,
But only common thieves and murderers to be captured and sentenced.
We cannot raise them to the rank of opponent, but only see them clear
As a rabble frightened of the world and of those who do not fear them.
For we do not fear them, and we see them as small & brutish criminals,
As mere gangs of killers doomed to spend the rest of their days in cells.
Someday it may be that we use our wit to find ways beyond these jails,
And when that day arrives I will be the first to celebrate and salute it,
Because we will finally have discovered the country beyond violence,
That country we have so desired and so long and so fruitlessly sought,
But meanwhile here we are faced with immense trials and tribulations,
Yet intent on accomplishing a victory beyond the minds of murderers.

There are, it may be, many months of fiery trial & sacrifice ahead of us.
It is a fearful thing to lead this great peaceful people into this new war,
A war unlike any we have heretofore fought, a war against a grim clan
Who have without compunction roasted children, and then applauded;
But I tell you clearly tonight that there is one way only to win this war,
Not with bullets but with brains, not with bombing but with brilliance.
The right is more precious than peace, and we are charged to defend it,
And we fight, as we always have, for those things that we dearly love,
For the concert of free peoples as shall bring peace & safety to all men;
But we do so with a new sword, more terrible and sharp than any ever,
The whip of our wits, powered not by muscle but by a ferocious heart.

In His Wallet after the Terrorist Bombing

Three library cards, all tattered—college, city, county.
Driver's license in which he looks about ten years old.
Grocery store club membership cards, all bright colors.
Photograph of his three children when they were small.
Photo of his wife which he liked for her exuberant grin
But she hated because the blue dress made her look fat.
Blood donation card. Eleven donations in a single year
And then nothing for seven years. Man, *there's* a story.
Gym membership card, never used, clearly promotion.
Major credit card with a piece of white athletic tape on
It on which someone, presumably him, had written **DO
NOT USE!** A gift card past its due date for a bookstore.
The invaluable American Automobile Association card.
A warranty for the septal occluder implanted in his son.
Why he would carry around a warranty card no one can
Explain, said his wife, but that's *exactly* his personality.
Not one but three gift cards to expensive men's clothes
Stores, which the fact that they were not used also says
A lot about him, said his wife. I bet they're all expired.
A total of eight insurance cards for the two family cars.
He never, and I mean *never*, threw away any insurance
Item whatsoever, said his wife, and not because he was
Meticulous but the complete reverse, total manic fright
That he would throw a card or a receipt away and then
He would suddenly be liable for seven million dollars.
A complete and utter financial paranoiac. On the other
Hand he never did miss a payment over all these years.

A video store card for a chain which went bust several
Years ago; he thought it might be resurrected, so there
You go, he'd be ready. This was also what he was like.
Medical and dental insurance cards for all the children.
Organ donation card on which he had written *the brain
Goes to the Republican Party, distribute as necessary.*
A scrap of red paper with the kids' cell phone numbers.
Three blank checks. A scrap of paper with his wedding
Vows in bold type, underlined by hand. A set of tickets
To a concert two months from now. A brief email from
A woman in another country, responding to something
He had written after September 11, and this note, from
A Muslim woman, is worth quoting. *The terrorists did
A wrong despicable thing, never would any of Muslim
Ever think of harming another human being. This isn't
Nor will it ever be a part of Muslim. I vow this is truth.*

Aequus

I cannot explain adequately or articulately how much it matters to me
That the elderberry bush by the back porch came back to life this year.
Somehow I just didn't think it would. I know this is my problem, lack
Of faith, a kind of expectation that things will dissolve, a dry certainty
Of entropy, and believe me I have lectured myself about it, and ranted
And raved to everyone else, and published and performed on the topic,
I have been relentlessly and incredibly boring about hope and suchlike,
But there I am, in the halting stammering sunlight on equinox morning,
Hammered by savage green elderberry tongues all ravenous for the sun.
You couldn't stop them if you tried. You could chop down every spine,
Hack up the roots, roast it all to pale and shameful ash, and up it comes
Again desperate and thirsty and caring not at all who you think you are.
I cannot explain adequately or articulately how much this matters to me.
I didn't think it would happen. The times are dark. Hope is in full flight.
Hope is a refugee always on the road with no shoes or milk for the baby.
You can't trust that a love will keep sending up these mad green arrows.
But there is the bush all defiant and careless on the morning of equinox.
Equinox, from the Latin *aequus* and *nox*, equal and night. Isn't *that* apt,
That whenever you think the dark has won the day leaps out rebellious?

On Meeting George Cardinal Pell,
the Archbishop of Sydney in Australia,
Outside His Office in Saint Mary's Cathedral,
and Falling into Gabbling with His Eminence

About all sorts of things, primarily and foremost my American accent,
Which didn't seem all that undiluted or impenetrable to me, personally,
But us guys from Ballarat, as he said, sound like we are from Chicago,
Which set us off conversing about how some accents are utterly eerily
Exactly the same as other accents, such as in my experience New York
Accents, say accents from Hell's Kitchen or lower Brooklyn, are oddly
The same as accents from central New Orleans, which doesn't calculate,
But it makes you wonder, doesn't it? Indeed it does, said His Eminence,
Looming over me like he was nine feet tall. When I was a Ballarat boy,
We took pleasure in trying to discern accents from the west, or the city.
In the way of boys we thought we were terrific at guessing provenance
But I suspect we were not quite as excellent at it as we thought we were.
This seems to me an essential law of the human condition, that we think
We are better than we are, which, in a real sense, explains my vocation.
He smiled down from his vast height and we shook hands and went off
Each to his own muddled and happy existence, but I have often thought
Of that conversation, and not because of his excellent roaring red sash,
You hardly ever see a guy ambling around proudly with a scarlet sash,
Or because he is the wry and intelligent and just a little tiny bit arrogant
Cardinal archbishop of the most beautiful city on the God-given planet,
But because I never heard a pithier explanation of why there are priests.
Kind of cut right to the chase. I told him his remark was kind of a koan,
I would ramble it over and over in my mind like a prism, and he smiled.

Driving the Dalai Lama to Seattle

Or here's a story. A cheerful young man tells it over coffee.
A year ago I drove the Dalai Lama from Portland to Seattle,
He says. He finished a speech here and had to rush up north
For the next one, but planes and trains weren't running so I
Volunteered to drive him and he said sure, that'd be terrific,
So off we go whipping up the interstate. I asked him to rest
In the back seat, maybe stretch out and read, or catch a nap,
But he said no, he liked trees and hills and rivers and birds,
So he sat up front and fiddled with the radio the whole trip.
Well, you wouldn't *believe* that man's knowledge of music.
It began with Paul Revere and the Raiders, which he loved,
And then riffed off into the Shins and Fountains of Wayne,
And the Surfaris and Ventures, he's totally into surf music,
And Link Wray and Robert Gordon, he loooves rockabilly,
And even esoteric stuff like Arvo Pärt and Kronos Quartet.
It was hilarious. By the time we passed the Lewis River he
Was five bucks up on me in bets who could name the song
First. You wouldn't believe this guy. Give him three notes
And he's got the song, nine out of ten times. No way can I
Explain how funny this was. I was totally losing it laughing.
And his face, man, when he shouted something like *Bruce!*
It was one of those trips you did not want it to ever be over.
We finally pull into Seattle, and of course it's raining hard,
And I get out the nine bucks I owe him from the bets I lost,
And he won't take the money, he says give it to some kids,
And then he says, still smiling, that of course the reason he
Knows seven million songs is that he is always on the road,

36

A line I never forgot, and a line that makes you sort of sad,
When you think about it. The poor guy, his country stolen,
His family and friends in exile or dead, everybody nodding
At what he says about compassion but no one really does it,
How he can be so real and funny I haven't the faintest idea.
But I tell you, don't bet against the guy knowing Dick Dale
Or They Might Be Giants or Midnight Oil or Willie Nelson.
Trust me when I tell you he's the one guy *not* to bet against.

Martin King Playing Baseball on St. Helena Island, South Carolina, Late in the Year of Our Lord 1967

A decent ballplayer, good bat great glove,
Given to trash-talking in his younger days
But marinated now in passions and pains,
He positions himself in shallow right field
And contemplates the roaring of the hours.
Behind him looms the ancient hungry sea.
The voices of his aides tatter in the breeze.
Today he cannot wear a thin black necktie,
This was the condition laid down by aides,
Today he is not Dr. Martin Luther King Jr.
But the calm boy christened Michael King
By his mama until his papa saw fit and apt
To rename both himself and his oldest son
When the boy was six. All his young years
Michael was a ballplayer, quick and tough,
Usually stationing himself at short or third
As those were the positions of opportunity
And captaincy, a job he claimed even then.
Only later, on days like this, on St. Helena
Where his aides haul him for resurrections,
Does he lope out to roam the rippled grass,
The sprawling patient ocean of the outfield,
Where he hums a little, ponders his women,
Ponders the confusing glory of his children,
Worries if he will make it even to age forty,
Ponders the nature and bone of a weariness

So deep that he weeps when he is left alone.
But then suddenly baseball's loveliest song,
A bat snapping whipquick against a fastball,
And he jumps, instantly, doesn't even think,
Toward where he absolutely knows it went,
His body remembering every steaming holy
Game he ever played, every pickup and peg,
Every knob of every bat, every shred of joy.
Sometimes I wish he'd had a baseball glove
On his hand that next spring, on the balcony,
You wish someone had handed him a glove
To sign, or as a goof, so that he'd have it on
When there was that sudden cracking sound
And a bullet flew right at the knot of his tie;
With a mitt on he might have been Michael
Sprinting instantly and unconsciously away.
And what if he did, you know what I mean?
What if he did? Perhaps he would plummet
From view, his philandering on cable news,
Financial improprieties, the usual scandals,
But maybe not. Maybe his insane throbbing
Idea would have rooted in the soils of souls.
Maybe people in this bruising holy country
Would laugh and shake their heads that we
Ever killed people over races and religions,
Maybe people would be saying, old Martin,
Good thing he was a hell of a baseball man
When he was a kid, you know what I mean,
Good thing he knew how to evade a rocket.
Maybe a lot of people would be saying that.

Lines on Watching Game Two
of the 1986 Celtics vs. Bulls Playoff Series
Twenty-Two Years Later in a Motel in Michigan

For reasons having to do initially with cable access and ESPN Classic,
But then increasingly for reasons having to do with the stunning grace
And ferocity of the game, the violent creativity of the players, the deft
Sleight of hand, the incredible changing of paces and shifting of gears,
The infinitesimal advantage to be earned by a sudden elbow to a throat,
The astounding ease with which a man on the ground is instantly aloft,
The intently relaxed way a man far from the basket just snaps his wrist
And the ball leaps away in a perfect looping arc to the heart of the hole,
The way men angle and spin and collide and cut and screen and chatter,
The half-grins, the snarls, the wrenching of coachly hair, the basso wits
Of the centers cursing, the way a panthery young man drives the action
Despite the fact that he is a kid, all of twenty-three years old, too young
To be jaded or weary, too young to not smile broadly occasionally, just
Because this is such an unbelievably great game, it turns out this is one
Of the greatest games there ever was, a rising team just starting to sense
Its own mettle and muscle against the best team in the world that spring,
And I end up watching the entire game for the second time, two decades
Apart, the first time I was in my twenties too, lean and lithe and foolish.
The Celtics win this one in overtime, Michael dropping a still-record 63
On the champs, and the channel moves along to some other past heroics,
But I find myself curiously moved. It's just a game, in the end, and what
Matters is kids and pain and grace and cramming war back into the hole
From which it was hatched when we came down terrified from the trees.
But games are wars, you know, wars we have carved into grace and joy,
Wars bent into a shape where collisions don't mean skulls on iron pikes;

And just for a minute, there in a motel in Michigan, I think maybe sport
Means more than we know. Maybe we are headed to a home we did not
Know we had. Maybe the little things that make us happy are directions.

To the United Airlines Signalman
Silently Reading the New Testament
in an Alcove Under the Extendable Jetway
at Gate C-9 in Chicago on a Morning in April

Sir, that book has absorbed me also, riveted me utterly sometimes,
And I am never sure where exactly to rank it among literary glories.
On the one hand you can with wry confidence say that it's the most
Influential collection of stories ever published, more so maybe than
The prequel, though the First Book appeared long before the sequel,
But on the other hand you could with the same inarguable assurance
Say that it has caused a million murders & been the proximate spark
Of battles, arguments, debates, tortures, crusades, and many other sins
Uncountable except by the Mercy to whom it is assuredly dedicated.
In a sense it is a quest narrative, the tale of a young man on the road,
Always walking, answering questions with questions, a gnomic guy,
Fond of odd metaphors, losing his temper here and there, a parablist,
Accompanied by what you have to admit is a real chaotic entourage,
Fishermen, tax-collectors, tent-makers, roadies, a few brave women
Who paid for things and made arrangements, and the *crowds*—man,
You wouldn't believe the bustle and burble of folks massing against
The fence to catch a glimpse of the guy, to hear a snatch of what He
Had to say, remember Zacchaeus hoisting himself into the sycamore
Tree? There must have been hundreds of people like old Zacchaeus,
Catching a shred of that voice at the edge of the crowd, going home
Wondering. And they told someone else, who told someone, and he
Wrote it down a little, that third man, and somewhere along the line
Someone brilliant and intent and perhaps inspired by a music we do
Not have words for, sat down and stitched all those stories together,

And then persuaded his sister or his cousin to write a copy or seven,
And those were copied, and because they thought Luke or Matthew
A saintly guy they named the books for him, and there were debates
And fistfights and worse about which books were formally inspired,
And eventually there came to be a book which a thin man is reading
Under the jetway in Chicago. We talked for a moment, the lean man
And me, about this most remarkable book, *I reads it each every day*,
He said, smiling, and afterwards I thought not only how terrifying it
Is that a book like this or the Qurʾan can lead to the murder of kids,
But how astonishing it is, how truly unbelievable, that a book can be
Alive after all these years, can have in its fragile pages that one man,
Dusty and complicated, tart and testy, tired and afraid, unforgettable.

Sayyida

Or here's a story. A young priest tells it with wonder on his face.
One night I get a call from the hospital and a young girl is dying,
He says. I sprint to the hospital but when I get there she has died.
Her parents are both Muslims and both of them are really young.
I ask what's the girl's name and the mother says *she was Fatima*.
Even right there I noticed and remarked to myself the verb tense,
Isn't that crazy, the things you notice when you are at the abyss?
I anoint the palms of her hands with oil but before I start prayers
I say to the parents we all believe that the Lady is the last refuge,
That Mary is the mother of us all, with her all things are possible,
So let us join hands and beg life back into this innocent holy girl.
Sayyida, says the father, *Lady, I beg our baby back from the end,*
And then there was about a minute with no sound except beeping
From the machine and the mother crying, and then, I kid you not,
The girl opened her eyes. I mean, even I was speechless, and I'm
A professional believer in miracles, you know? The father kneels
Down and puts his head against the cold linoleum floor and weeps
And weeps and weeps. The mother cradles her baby. I stand there
With my mouth hanging open like a fish. We don't have language
That fits most of what is, that's what I think. Words are real weak.
But you remember that word when things are dark. *Sayyida. Lady.*

What People Say When They Mean Something Other Than What They Say

I have become a broken student of things people say
When they mean something other than what they say.
I have been dealing with some things meant pregnant.
God gives all sorts of gifts meant an autistic daughter.
Trying to get centered meant finding a halfway house.
A little time off meant walking to the police station to
Hand over the rifle he had spent the whole night with,
Staring at the barrel, a shoelace attached to the trigger,
And the police officer on duty at eight in the morning,
Who had weirdly served in the same platoon in a war,
Gently took the rifle and checked the safety and came
Around the desk and wrapped his arm around the guy
And walked him down to the little park by the library,
Where they sat and talked for hours. *Jarheads jawing,*
That was the phrase the policeman used when he told
Me the story, and he said it with a smile, but he knew
And I knew that what he said isn't at all what he said.

Our Dear Leader

Pol Pot christened himself Brother Number One.
Mao Tse-tung named himself the Great Helmsman.
Joseph Stalin, whose original surname means garbage,
Named himself all sorts of things, like Man of Steel,
And Koba, the name of the hero in a popular novel.
Benito Mussolini named himself Il Duce, The Leader.
Kim Jong Il made everyone call him Our Dear Leader,
And called himself the Mighty Man from the Mountain.
His dad Kim Il-Sung called himself The Great Leader
And arranged that he be named President for Eternity
Even after he was mausoleumed and worshippable.
Osama son of Mohammed son of Awad son of Laden
Preferred to be called The Director or the Lion Sheik.
Saparmyrat Ataýewiç Nyýazow of Turkmenistan
Made it a law that he be addressed as The Leader.
Also he named a meteorite for himself, renamed
The days of the week and the months of the year,
And renamed bread for his late lamented mother.
Muammar al-Gaddafi called himself Brother Leader.
Idi Amin Dada called himself Conqueror of the British
Empire in Africa in General and Uganda in Particular,
And God help the soul who didn't use the Initial Caps.
Saddam Hussein had one million paintings of himself
Distributed throughout Iraq. Also thousands of statues.
You wouldn't believe how many Fathers of the Country
There have been, how many Glorious National Heroes.
You have to wonder what twists and frightens a boy so
That he spends the rest of his life wearing a hero mask
And killing people to prove that they love him dearly.

At the Football Players' Table

Or here's a story. There was a guy who played football in high school.
Every day all the football players sat together at two tables in the back.
As at most high schools the lunchroom was divided into tiny countries
With the studious in one corner and socialites in another and the geeks
The usual total free agents when it comes to finding a spot to eat lunch.
The stoners of course are outside under the bleachers trying to be cool.
Anyway in this school there are a few retarded kids, this was years ago
Before the words developmentally disabled were invented, and there's
One retarded girl who gets to lunch late, she is not having the best day,
And she gets her tray and looks in vain for a place to sit down, and she
Sees a spot open at the football players' table, the halfback ate and ran,
And, not comprehending the intricate laws of power and rank, she sits.
One of the football players, a lunk who will remember this moment all
His life, makes a cutting remark and shoves her plastic tray to the floor.
The girl sits quiet, all too familiar with the words and the sneering tone.
Another boy at the table rises, picks up the tray, brings it to the kitchen,
Loads another tray, carries it to the table, sets it before the startled girl,
And sits back in his own chair, staring at his teammate. Nobody makes
A sound. Years later this boy who picked up the tray will be murdered
On September 11, roasted to death in the towers by a celebrating thug,
And the kid who used to be a lunk says to the reporter from the *Times*,
You want to know about my buddy? I'll tell you a story about one day
Years ago at school where I saw for the first time what a hero really is.

Learning Aramaic

There really was a guy named Yeshua bin Yusuf, of course, some years ago.
That was his real name, Jesus the son of Joseph, in the language many of us
Speak now, a language that wasn't spoken then. The language that we speak
Now was being invented on a wet island between the lands of Gaul and Eire.
Yeshua, however, spoke Aramaic, a language that is fading away these days.
But a few people still speak it. A girl from Syria tells me a couple of phrases
To say if I want to have the words the Christ spoke in the cave of my mouth.
Awafih, she says, smiling, that means hello, he certainly said that a lot, don't
You think? and *alloy a pelach a feethah*, that means God be with you, mostly
We say that on greeting and parting, so I am pretty sure he said that probably
A hundred times a day. You try it. Say it with feeling. I am pretty sure he did.

In Isolation Room Three of the Home for Boys Who Had Unimaginable Crimes Committed upon Them

The walls are a brilliant fresh green, the color of blackberry shoots
In March, you know what I mean, when they first emerge like tiny
Crowns for tiny kings, they are a shade of green that you could *eat*.
Green herons are that green sometimes, and violet-green swallows,
They are too, a luminescent green like a signal from another planet.
And sailors see green like that on old mother sea when the sun dies.
You wonder who decided to paint the walls the greenest green ever.
I bet no one picked this color because it was found to be restorative
Or anything psychological like that, I bet no one consulted a report
On color and healing, I bet no committee or study picked this color.
I bet the guy who painted this room just somehow knew what to do.
Sometimes, every once in a while, not very often, not often enough,
We know what to do. Maybe this brilliant green is how we get there.

A Mass

One night a quiet old priest tells me a story.
I was in China for many long years, he says,
Then as now thorny years for all concerned,
But there were moments of surpassing grace.
I'll tell you one. One night I was summoned
To a baptism. The young father came for me.
We slipped silently through long dark alleys.
I remember a heavy fog and mist and smoke.
The baby had been born in an old bathroom.
The young mother slept exhausted in the tub.
Her mother, all of maybe forty, stood watch.
In the course of the baptism the mother says
That she had not witnessed a Mass for thirty
Years, since she was a small child in Hunan.
Well, I hesitated a long moment, I must say.
If we had been caught we'd all die in prison,
But isn't a chance like that the whole point?
So we had a lightning Mass in the bathroom.
Crusts of bread, water from the tap as wine,
Five congregants all told, two sound asleep.
For all the hard moments of my years there,
For all the disappointments and exhaustion,
That happened, and that's about everything.
Do you know what I am trying to say here?

As I Ever Saw

Or here's a story. A young mother tells it.
We are talking about bravery and courage,
Grace under duress, that's all that matters,
And she tells me that once, in the hospital,
She saw bravery as close as you can see it.
There was a kid, she said, he was like four
Years old, and he had a really evil disease,
And he was totally wiped, he couldn't get
Any more exhausted, been in bed a month
Solid, couldn't even walk to the bathroom,
And one day a volunteer art teacher walks
In and asks do you want to paint and such,
And the kid, who can hardly spit, says ya!,
And hauls himself up to sitting, and paints
For an hour, and asks questions, and sings
Songs, and helps put beads on a necklace,
And when the teacher leaves, he collapses
Back in the bed and didn't move for days.
He said yes just to make that teacher glad,
I'm absolutely sure of it. You want brave?
That kid was as brave a kid as I ever saw.

A Note on the Way a Tiny Baby Girl Startles with Delight as Her Weary Young Dad Carts Her by Victor Brauner's Painting *Prelude to a Civilization* at the Met One Afternoon

As I sit staring at the shoes and boots and socks and slippers of passersby,
The lovely clothing of their tired feet more of a creative accomplishment
Than a whole hell of a lot of the paintings, seems to me, but I know zero,
I just savor what is, and am just not hip enough to savor witty comments
On the exhausted artistic tradition or the postness of the postpostmodern.

I like faces and cats and shoes and stables and the dog in the background.
I like the push-broom and sweeping-pan of the janitor and his green shirt.
I like the three newspapers folded in quarters in his left rear pants pocket,
And I like that I can make out they are the *Post*, the *News*, and the *Times*.
I like that no one seems to notice as he works silently near Georges Rouault.

I like the design of the electrical outlets, the yawns of the security guards,
The thoughtful placement of the heat vents & the unobtrusive thermostats.
I like the scuff-pattern in the carpet and how this shows the flow of traffic.
I like the tiny screws with which art is crucified to the wall and how paint
Is meticulously painted over the screw-tops so that you have to look close

To see the screws and the wires and the brackets and the inarguable bolts.
I mean, I love a lot of the work held in this most polite and expensive zoo,
A lot of it is absolutely stunning and brave and wild, like Ibram Lassaw's
Incredible wire apartment building, and Ilia Repin's painting of his friend
Vsevolod Mikhailovich Garshin, and Yves Tanguy's dream of the future,

And to see Van Gogh's maniacal dense oil up close is to pray for the guy,
But the coolest sweetest piece of art I saw that day was this tiny baby girl

Dreaming on her daddy's neck as he ambled past that epic Victor Brauner
And her face lit up like a song, she wriggled and chortled and laughed out
Loud, and everybody stopped and smiled. Boy, talk about a masterpiece!

On 155th Street,
in the Borough of Manhattan,
in the Seething City of New York,

A girl in a wheelchair is being towed up the steep hill to Broadway
By a guy maybe her brother or her boyfriend, both of them dressed
For the formal reception they just escaped & both of them laughing
So hard that I start laughing too, you know what I mean, irresistible
Giggling, and he's working like a mule, he's working like Sisyphus
In reverse, his suit jacket and tie flapping in the breeze, her flowery
Dress rippling, she's holding onto his right arm with both her hands
And he's pumping his knees like a fullback against gravity's tackle,
And by God if he doesn't do it, he hauls her all the way to the light,
Where he bends over to catch his breath and her shrieks of laughter
Are about the coolest sound I ever heard in all my born and blessed
Days. I have heard a lot of extraordinary things in my life, my sons'
First sucks, my daughter's mewling, a woman saying quietly *yes* on
A hill by the sea, the shuffle of snow, the wheedle of thrushes, owls
Murmuring to each other, roaring music, last words, newborn songs,
But the sweet shards of that girl's laughter up at the top of the street:
Man, I was lucky enough, or chosen, to hear that, and I mutter *amen*.

Near Musa Qala

Or here's a story. A cheerful young man tells it.
He is just returned from one of our current wars.
We were not allowed to get involved in civilian
Matters overmuch but sometimes you just were,
He says, that's basically the point of being there
When you think about it. Well, one time I drove
A load of school kids from one town to another,
It's a long story, there were like nine or ten kids
In my truck bouncing around crazily back there,
I could hear them laughing whenever I hit holes
Which I was doing on purpose to get the laughs,
You know how you do that with kids and trucks,
And then I noticed a gang of F-16s headed right
To where I was going. These are Falcons, major
Weaponry, where they go you do not want to be.
I didn't even need to radio in, man, I knew what
Was up so I pull over and yell at the kids *lie flat!*
I mean we're basically safe, the jets are targeted
Elsewhere and they vanish but what I remember
Is that incredible silence in the back of the truck.
Those kids were terrified, boy, and that was safe
As they were going to get that day that's for sure.
Well, there was no point in going on to the town,
Probably most of the town wasn't there anymore
Anyways so we turn around and go back quietly.
People think that what you remember from wars
Is the bombing and shooting and all that, but my
Experience is, it's moments in between that stay
With you a long time after. I guess I'll find out.

This Wild World

Well, here's the story of stories, the mother of all stories.
A girl, nine months pregnant, decides to marry the father
Of her child or children. They hurriedly and happily make
Arrangements with a cheerful and understanding minister,
And they parade, attended by those they love, to the altar,
Whereupon, having just assented publicly to the marriage,
She goes into labor, and delivers not one but two children,
A girl and a boy, at the tiny shrine dedicated to the Virgin.
You couldn't make this up if you tried. The father, twenty,
Cries. The mother, to her eternal credit, laughs and laughs.
The minister, astonished by nothing after a riveting career,
Cuts the umbilical cord, hugs the dad, baptizes the infants,
Cups that mother's face in his huge hands and blesses her,
And ambles cheerfully back to the kitchen to make coffee.
Now isn't that about the best story ever in this wild world?

A Note on Vocabulary in the Cardiometabolic Field

Where I am wandering one afternoon thinking of my second son who not once
But twice had a surgeon's fingers milling through the muscle of his wild heart.
Eleven years ago now. He doesn't remember those hours, my boy, but I sure do.
His chicken chest gaping open like a mouth. Me eating a word like *septectomy*
For breakfast, bending it this way and that, trying to find any way to get inside.
Situs solitus and *ventricular inversion* and *tricuspid hypophasia* and *anastamosis*
Ranged across the horizon like the most incredible and unimaginable mountains.
Who ever thought there would be a time when we could remember those times?
But here we are on the other side of the mountains, and of all things to see what
Do we see? Mountains beyond mountains and yet more mountains beyond them.
We have such an itch for pattern and narrative, such a ravenous hunger for order,
But there is no pattern, there is no order, there isn't really even a hint of coherent
Narrative shape, the fact of the matter is that at best we maunder forward with all
Possible grace in the moments when we are not thrashing and sobbing and crazy.
Believe me, I know about thrashing and sobbing and crazy, he's a teenager now,
Arrogant as sin one moment and weeping from the bottom of his bones the next,
Making everyone weep with laughter one day and roar with fear and fury another.
Mountains beyond mountains and yet further mountains beyond those mountains.
I used to think if we could just get through this time everything will be peaceful,
At least we won't be terrified and exhausted, but it turns out there's lots and lots
Of ways to be terrified and exhausted, who knew? So hold my hand and let's go
Up this next mountain. Who cares about other mountains? Isn't this one lovely?

Question: If a Shark Eats a Seal, Does the Soul of the Seal Go into the Soul of the Shark?

Asked of me in a fourth-grade class at Our Lady of Perpetual Inquisitiveness,
A class that had started out talking about literature, but then of course swerved
Right into sharks and crocodiles and dinosaurs and the dog that bit Ellen Anne,
This was a mountainous and amazing dog, it was as big as a car and could talk,
She said, it said curse words both before and after it chewed on my elbow, see?
Yeah, anyway, says another kid, his name is Harry, do bears have hairy souls?
Does a blue whale have a blue soul? Let's say a shark eats a seal, does the soul
Of the seal go into the soul of the shark? And do souls get, you know, excreted?
And what's the story with trees? If the tree can't move, does that mean its soul
Is stuck there too? And do souls get sick? Can a soul die before its person does?
And what if you lose your soul like at the airport? What if you get hit by a train,
Does your soul get knocked into the nearest person or a bird or an electric wire?
Can you get the wrong soul by accident? Is that why terrorist men are so angry?
If your parents get divorced, do their souls get marks on them? Are there really
Soul mates, or is that just something people say that doesn't mean what it says?
If the soul isn't attached to the body, then can something like a car have a soul?
What about trout? What about computers? What about the New York Yankees?
By now the classroom is seething and shouting and laughing and kids are rising
From their seats like souls are said to rise from the body. Even the teacher grins,
Despite or maybe because of the total eager chaos. One more question, yes, you
In the back row, what's your name? Felipe, says the lad, thin as a question mark.
After you die, can your soul go to any of the universes that ever were or will be?

The Bagpiper in the Last Row
of the Trolley in Massachusetts
Tells Stories about Epiphanies

I play the pipes only on the weekends, you know.
The rest of the time I teach music in kindergarten,
And for years I have been teaching your ordinary
Instruments, guitar and piano and fiddle and such,
Though of course no instrument is at all ordinary,
But you shoulda seen the kids gawk the morning
I strolled in wearing a kilt and blowing real loud!
I teach music in middle school down the shore too.
One time there was a boy I just could *not* connect,
You know what I'm saying? Nobody could get in,
And the doors were closing on this kid, real quick
He was going to be hopping from prison to prison,
And by God if the pipes didn't get him by the hair.
I was just practicing after school before driving up
To Maine to play a wedding and he comes around
The corner and he stops like someone slapped him.
The kid ended up being one unbe*liev*able bagpiper.
Stuff like that happens all the time, it seems to me,
But maybe there's so much of it that we get casual
About stuff like that always happening, am I right?

On Malolo Street, in Hanalei

A gentle man walking to the bus to Kilauea tells me
About the moment that his daughter returned to him.
There had been several dangerous and painful years,
He says, so gently that I can hardly hear his struggle.
There had been some very difficult and bitter events.
So one day she and I are walking way up in the hills.
It was a gathering to benefit a school, as I remember.
We had not spoken that day or indeed for some days.
She was walking ahead of me. I think she was thirty.
We were on the fringe of the swamp that is up there,
When she stopped and said, Papa! look, the puaiohi!
Which is a very shy thrush that lives only near there.
You can tell it is the puaiohi because of its pink legs.
We stood there happy for a minute and then went on.
Even then I was extra happy because she was happy,
And I had worried that so many bad times had taken
Away her well of happiness. You know what I mean
Because you are a father too, yes? We always worry.
That was about two years ago and things are healthy
Now. We will never be the best of friends, too much
Has happened, but we can talk and laugh again now,
And it seems to me that the little thrush was magical.
You know what I mean because you are a father also.

Maldestro

I am *proud* of being lefty, says my son, lefties are the coolest guys there *are*,
And you can't change that, you can't change me, you are not the boss of me,
And I say, hiding in the thicket of words as usual, trying to find calm footing,
Ah, left-handed, *sinistral* is the term, you know, *ciotog* as your forebears said
Back in ancient Ireland, and gauche is the word in the French, also maladroit,
Which has adopted another meaning in English as I am certain you are aware.
He glares at me, sure that I am ragging him in some stuffy scholarly dad way,
But now I am off and running, mostly because I am an idiot, but also because
I know that if I can get him to grin then we have some shaky common ground,
And I say *maldestro* is the Italian, I think, and *links* is lefty in the Netherlands,
And is there a cooler national name than that, the Under Lands, isn't that neat,
But anyway there's a whole pancultural thing with handedness and languages,
The left hand is bad form in Islam and Hinduism, it's considered most vulgar,
And the Portuguese word for lefty, *canhoto*, used to be the word used for devil.
In Chinese, Welsh, Norwegian, Hungarian, Australian, Russian, even in Latin,
It's a hard road being lefty, all the righties and all the languages your enemies;
But hey, in Esperanto there's no bad connotation to being left-handed, my boy,
So there you go, the future for you is the language for everyone, I suppose you
Will be working at the United Nations, or whatever shape that ancient impulse
Takes in your lifetime, and I wish you the best with that, and also I admire you.
He was about to say *whatever*, I know he was, I can tell from the set of his face,
The face I have studied for nearly fourteen years, but he's distracted by *admire*,
That caught him off guard, the hint of a compliment is annoying and confusing,
He's not sure where that was coming from and all compliments from dad smell
Like the preface to a lecture, in his experience, so he stomps off, and I sit there,
Weary, confused, in love, frightened, wondering what tenor of man he will be,
Wondering why the definitions of love are so often also the definitions of pain.
Ever it was thus, ever thus it will be, but more than anything else this morning,
More than anything, I wish he would run back and hug me again, just this once.

Things to Do If I Am Allowed to Get Ancient, Which Seems Unlikely, but You Never Know

Spend an entire morning tying and untying all sorts of nautical knots.
Spend an afternoon filling in every o in a Proust novel in the library,
And blessing the creativity of the great Scottish writer Alastair Reid,
Who conceived the idea, although he didn't specify that it be Marcel.
Spend an afternoon staring at a cedar tree and celebrating endurance.
Try to draw, with meticulous and ferocious attention, one blue heron.
Listen, and I mean totally intently listen, to any child, all blessed day.
Build, for God's sake, one birdhouse. Just the one. Not even sturdily.
Do like a late friend did and secretly plant thousands of trees on golf
Courses and in cemeteries and in circles in the lawns of good citizens.
Dismantle an ancient tool shed, with the utmost respect and affection.
Spend a day pumping basketballs and soccer balls at the playgrounds.
Spend a morning washing the windows of all odd-numbered houses.
Spend an evening tending bar at an Elks or Moose or Veterans lodge.
Get a haircut that leaves my head looking like a chessboard, and then
Knock on the back door of the house where my grandchildren reside,
And totally freak them out laughing hysterically at what grampa did!
Write, and then persuade some eager young nut to produce, one play.
Take one photograph a day of my wife's face, for one year or twenty,
As long as she is present and willing to be photographed, and as long
As I am capable of holding the camera or whatever medium will then
Be invented, and then go downstairs with the photograph of that day,
And paste it carefully into its position on the wall with all its fellows,
And stand back to get a good look at all the different women she was,
All those one days after another, never one the same, every one sweet
And holy in its own incredible way, never to be repeated. Then kneel
Down, if I still can, which will be highly improbable, and say thanks.

62

What a Father Thinks While Driving
His Daughter, Age Seventeen, to Rehab

Are we not going to exchange a single word on this entire trip?
Maybe there was one moment, when she was a kid, say, seven,
When I said exactly the wrong word or didn't say the right one,
And everything spun off grim and inevitable from that moment,
Or maybe it was something I should have done and just did not,
Like after her first soccer game or the first time she failed a test,
There was a keening in her heart and I absolutely utterly punted.
Or hell, maybe it's because we used to be Irish. We're only sots.
Like your tribal people who can't drink either, the poor bastards.
Those poor people don't even get called the right name, do they,
Native Americans, American Indians, First Peoples, sweet Jesus,
No wonder they drink. Not to mention losing land and ancestors
To a bunch of people who invented new words for the robberies,
Manifest destiny, national expansion, sea to fecking shining sea.
Lord, the polite lies. Like rehabilitation, why not say drunk tank?
Seven miles to go. She's not going to speak or look at me or hug
Me today or any day ever again. Jesus, I was changing her diaper
Two minutes ago. Birthday cakes, kindergarten bus, cell phones,
Summer camp, ski trips, college admission viewbooks, do I save
Those or throw them in recycling? Are there visiting hours? Will
She die in there? Will she die out here? Did I love her mom more
Than her, is that the problem? Will they take plastic at the clinic?
Is there ever going to be a moment when I don't worry about her?
Are we ever going to sit on the grass again and laugh hysterically,
Laugh so hard our cheeks and stomachs ache and then totally lose
It laughing again just from the hilarious way the other one laughs?
I think those moments were the greatest moments there ever were
In the whole history of the whole world. Exit seventeen . . . this is it.

The Tenderness of It

You know what I miss? Changing diapers. Who would have thought
I would ever in a million years say such a thing, after a million hours
Changing diapers for three kids, two at the same time for a long time,
You never saw a happier guy that his kids finally figured out the drill
Except maybe a guy I know who his wife suddenly had triplets, girls,
This guy used to be a New York City homicide detective and he says
It was a hell of a lot easier being a detective than it is chasing the kids,
He says, you wouldn't believe how fast they move, and they *conspire*,
You know, he says, they give each other a look and then there's crime,
I complain about this to the wife, he says, but she says it's all my fault.
We talk about the wriggle and wrestle of it, the way odor is an assault,
About the motions and gestures of the ancient craft, and how you can
Do it without being all the way awake, and how the first few times are
Holy and confusing and then the next year is horrendous and tiresome,
But then after the kid starts figuring out the engineering of it all there's
A few times at the end when you are almost sort of nostalgic, you start
Savoring it, and realizing that you'll probably never do it again, unless
Someone loses her mind and itches for one last kid for female reasons,
And you spend those last weeks staring at your cool crazy naked child,
And rubbing your nose in her belly to make her make that walrus laugh,
And digging the scent of talcum powder, and admiring the brilliant guy
Who invented the deft fasteners on the edge of the diapers, and wonder
Whatever happened to diaper pins, did the corporations that make them
All go out of business or what, and dig the tiny foot-pedal on the bucket,
Making the lid of the bucket bang percussively until someone yells *stop!*
And just sort of swim in the tenderness of it all, you know what I mean?
I mean, it was frightening and astounding in the beginning, and then all

64

You wanted was to not be quite so familiar with the cost of handi-wipes,
And then without any fanfare it's gone forever, that tiny totally intimate
Moment between you and your kid, and you find yourself thinking, hey,
You know what, just for a day or two, I wouldn't mind changing diapers
Again, and hearing my kids giggle, and lifting them down from the table,
And watching them stagger off in redolent clouds of powder and burble;
But only for a day or two, let's not get crazy here, remember that *stench?*

On Watching a Brief Special Olympics Basketball Game during Halftime of the Usual Intense Professional Game

A muted conversational buzzle in the vast arena, a sort of tidal murmur.
The announcer announces the teams and there is a scattering of applause.
It's three on three, a team in green against a team in black, and my child
And I start to pay casual attention and then get riveted and soon I lose it,
For among the players there is a tall smiling boy who never gets the ball,
He moves gently around the lane with both arms raised high whether his
Team or the other has the ball, it doesn't seem to matter, he's not calling
For the ball or flashing that he's open, he just likes to hoist up his hands,
And he's so happy, his smile is so sweet and brilliant, he is so incredibly
Happy that something wrenches in me, something I can't stop or control,
And I sit in Section 111, Row M, Seat 12, my own boy carefully looking
In another direction, and just cry and cry. That's the happiest young man
I have ever seen, and he never gets the ball and he never *will* get the ball,
Ever, in his whole life, and he doesn't care, he just wants to float the lane
With his hands raised high. I cry and cry. My son, a wonderful basketball
Player, politely studies the game program and mows through his popcorn.
One guy on the black team scores all the points, and another guy takes 11
Shots and never once hits the rim, and a girl on the greens hits a long shot
And the crowd burbles for a few seconds, and the green team guy with the
Bald spot and the ponytail finally throws the ball to the boy with his arms
Up but the girl steals it and fires up one last errant shot before the buzzer,
And that's the game, both of the teams run off beaming and slapping five,
And still, no question about it, the happiest person on the face of the earth
Is that tall boy. I think he is maybe the Buddha or the Messiah or a genius.
Very soon the serious game will resume and I'll get a grip and get my cool
Back on, and my son will elbow me to see if it's okay for us to talk again,

And the world will spin on in its usual muddle and wonder, but once again
I have witnessed a being of light, once again I have been blessed by a child.
I think about that boy and his face the rest of the night and all this morning,
And now I hand him to you, beaming, both his hands raised high, *hallelujah!*

The Way the Light Was

One time I got stuck with my brother's girlfriend's kid brother,
This was while my brother and his girlfriend went to see a guy
About buying a convertible or some ridiculous excuse like that,
And after we mumbled at each other for a while, and pretended
To be interested in what the other guy said he was interested in,
We idly picked up baseball gloves and started whipping throws,
And it turned out that this kid who looked like king of the nerds
Had a real evil slider, an insane curve he could bend either way,
A sinker that fell off the table, a forkball, a screwball, and even,
By god, a split-fingered fastball which no one can throw except
Guys in the big leagues and not a whole lot of those guys either.
He even had a knuckleball which nearly smashed my spectacles
The one time it fluttered in like a fat bird with a terminal illness.
I asked him did he have a fastball as evil as the rest of his tools?
And he said yes but he hardly ever threw it because he was wild
With it, it was the one pitch he wasn't totally sure where it went.
I couldn't believe all this as we stood out there behind his house
Whipping the ball back and forth. He didn't even play the game,
Didn't much like baseball, he said, other guys ragged him when
He tried out, because he wasn't much of an athlete and couldn't
Hit for shit as he said, and because he looked like such a doofus
He never even got a tryout on the mound. I wish I could say that
I had some kind of epiphany right then and there, about illusions
And exteriors, appearance and reality, perception and exception,
But I didn't, partly because I just could not easily make the leap
Between the pimply shy kid winding up across the dappled yard
And the ball leaping out of his pudgy hand all eager and furious.

Man, what was that, forty years ago, I can't remember his name,
I can't even remember his sister's name so as to razz my brother,
But isn't it odd and amazing and puzzling and somehow crucial
That I remember the snap of his pitches, the way he very quietly
Muttered what he was throwing, the way he was so unbelievably
Good at something that he would never officially be any good at,
The way he furled and unfurled himself, the way the light was?

In the Homesteader Museum in Wyoming Just after an Unreal Early Fall Snowstorm

Which gives you a glint of a hint what it was like to live here
Without a furnace or electricity or heaters of any kind except
Each other or the horses or the pelt of bear and bison and elk,
& suggests the weary work of carving a life from the country:
Tractors, ditchers, planters, plows, threshers, graders, seeders,
No one ever talks about the *stuff* of homesteading, but by god
Here's a whole block devoted to toolery and machinery, each
Piece having to be cleaned & repaired, hauled and overhauled;
It's a monument to metals here, to our wonderful wit in wood.
I stand inside Ora Bever's cabin, built when the melted snows
Off Cedar and Rattlesnake mountains were first being herded
Into water for the big valley, and the Shoshone and Cheyenne
And Arapahoe and Crow people were finally being processed
Into camps, much like German prisoners would be years later
Here, and Americans of Japanese descent under the mountain
To the north, Heart Mountain, Ora Bever must have seen that
Mountain every day of her life, as she walked out to the cows,
Or set to breaking ice in the trough; and for an instant, a flash
Of something when there's no time between her time and this
Time, I *get* Ora Bever, her skinny shoulders, her wild temper,
The way she prayed and pondered all day long, dogs and dirt,
Metaphysics and religions, politics and geology, how a Crow
Woman would sing when the geese first flew over in autumn,
And how her song would bring winter trailing its white robes.
She knew a lot, Ora Bever did, in her house the size of a shed.
She knew more about a thousand things than I could imagine

Even not knowing. The reverse is true, of course, and in such
Stuff as insurance and old movies and professional basketball
Old Ora Bever can't hold my candle, you know what I mean?
And all this muck about how Americans used to be forthright
And tough and stalwart and tall but now are listless lazy liars
Addicted to electronics and caffeine and sex and credit cards,
That's a straw man disproved by a host of brave and gracious
Citizens, more than I can count in fifty years of being startled
By the generosity and creativity and humor of the Americans;
But here I stand, alone in the museum in the Big Horn Valley,
Wondering if we are as much advanced from Ora Bever's day
As we think we are. We wouldn't go back there for a moment,
Not one of us, except those nutty re-enactors, or a reactionary
Control freak peeved at the present and terrified of tomorrow,
But she sure saw the world with a hard immediacy that maybe
We miss more than we know. It comes at a mighty high price,
That access to the naked world, as you can see in Ora's cabin,
Not to even get into what it must have been like for the Crow;
But it's a cost I hope we always have the nuts and guts to pay.

Peter

One time when we were in Florida visiting my parents,
My three living brothers and my sister and I, all adults
Or seeming to be so, there was a moment in the garage
When my lengthy brother Peter was wielding a broom
And I said to him as I shuffled by, *hey, you okay, man?*
There's like some quiet sad thread in your face, and he
Started to cry, and he didn't say anything, but just kept
Sweeping, and I didn't say anything, but just put a paw
On his back, and we stayed like that for a moment, and
I was so overwhelmed with love for him that I shivered.
I don't have words that come anywhere near explaining
Anywhere near how I felt then, and have felt all my life,
About my kid brother. I mean, I could tell you hundreds
Of anecdotes about the past, how we laughed and fought,
How we went everywhere on our bicycles, how we wore
Our hair the same way, how we eventually wanted to be
So different, but for once the stories don't catch a whole
Hell of a lot of the power of the feeling I cannot explain.
I love him so much that sometimes it hurts to think of it.
Isn't that funny, that sometimes we love people so much
That we have to not think about them just to keep going?

At Herbert Hoover Elementary

There's stories and stories, and then there are little tiny stories
That make you want to sit down and laugh until your stomach
Aches and your cheeks ache and you think you maybe twisted
Your back somehow laughing. Like this one: There's a school
Where a kid, age five, out in the far thickets of the playground,
Finds a baby skunk, and he is so thrilled he crams it in his coat
And runs back to the classroom, but he's late for alphabet soup
So he pops it into his lunch bag and crams it in the refrigerator,
But then of course he totally and utterly forgets about the baby,
Because he's five and remembering his name is a chancy thing,
And late in the afternoon, after all the kids have sprinted home,
Of course the teacher opens the bag and the skunk tumbles out,
But the animal is all woozy and addled from being refrigerated,
So it just lies there and the teacher thinks it's dead, so she carts
It home to show her husband who is a zoologist, and the skunk
Wakes up in the warmth of the car and freaks, perhaps because
Of that awful music you play in the car, no wonder the creature
Was terrified, says the husband later, after he has calmed every
One down, cleaned the car, put iodine on her scratches, and put
The skunk on the porch with a bowl of milk and a beach towel,
All arranged inside the box in which the new refrigerator came.
You see, he says, trying to make her laugh, everything is about
Refrigeration, that's your lesson plan for tomorrow, what think?

Chen Yi

A tiny woman from China tells a story.
She tells the story outside in the wind.
It was a windy day like this when they
Arrived to take me to the prison camp,
She says. There were five Red Guards.
I took my violin, hiding it in a red bag
In which we carried a few possessions.
At camp, we grew rice and vegetables.
We weren't allowed to wear our shoes.
One task was to build a military tower.
I carried rocks to the mountain all day.
I was allowed to wear shoes that week.
I had my violin wrapped in my blanket.
I would practice fingering and bowing
At night, playing songs without music.
Then they let me play music outdoors,
But only revolutionary songs, but they,
The soldiers, I mean, just boys, really,
Only knew the words and the melody,
You see, so I could toy with melodies
As much as I wanted and no one knew.
That made it a great deal of fun for me.
I suppose this was my first composing.
The soldiers never realized what I did.
One day soldiers came for me and told
Me I had been chosen for the orchestra.
They would not allow me to say goodbye

For fear that others would try to escape.
The next week I was the concertmaster
Of the Opera. But still many years later
I practice fingering and bowing at night,
In my bed in the dark. I suppose there is
A part of me that will always be in camp.

On Absaroka Street

A man in Wyoming tells me a story. He is wearing an enormous hat
And sipping coffee and slowly going through a mountain of receipts.
He is an accountant, he says, what you would call a white-collar job,
But as you see, today it is an orange-collar profession for yours truly.
I guess this is a genetic thing for me, he says, working with the mind.
There is some family history that perhaps leads me to this profession.
My great-great-grandfather, here is a famous story about him, that he
Had just the worst eyesight in the world, so he spent all his time right
Around the village where he knew where everything was, and his job
Was to be the shaman—basically, both doctor and spiritual visionary.
We are the *Panátĭ*, the People, though we are referred to as Shoshone
By white people in general and historians and anthropologists and all.
Anyway in 1870 or so my great-great-grandfather somehow procured
A pair of spectacles, eyeglasses, and this was, as you can imagine, the
Most stunning and wonderful event, he could actually *see* his patients,
See the mountains on the horizon, recognize people who strolled past,
Easily distinguish one plant from another in the forest, make out stars,
And a hundred other small things that are not small at all for the blind
Or essentially blind, as he was. But then one day by accident he broke
Them, both the lenses shattered beyond repair. But here is the essence
Of my brave great-great-grandfather: he continued to wear the frames,
And he apparently continued to have the sharpest eyesight imaginable.
Now, whether this was miraculously so, or people believed it to be so,
Or he performed miracles of memory, or he perfectly imitated the gait
And habit of a man who had the eyesight of an eagle, none ever knew,
But he lived the rest of his life able to distinguish the tiniest difference
Between plants, and catch the faintest flicker of a patient's expression,

And point out vast intricate patterns among the stars to small children,
Among whom was, when he was a small boy, my grandfather, he who
Also became both a doctor and a minister, though in the white fashion.
So there is a good story for you today. Tell that to anyone you want to.
Stories like to travel, you know, just like people. They get restless too.

On Watching the Touch Football Game
in the Murk of an Early Autumn Evening

Down at the dark end of the street where the fir trees brood and rule.
No one has cut down a tree down there since before Christ was born.
There are two shrill tiny kids who have to cover each other of course.
Looks like the famous west coast offense with lots of guys in motion.
One kid goes out for a pass and cuts and slips and flails into the mud.
Everybody else loses it laughing helplessly for like two minutes until
The mud kid gets so angry he looks like he might cry or worse stomp
Off home in a high huff but they wheedle him back and throw to him
The next three times one of which he catches spectacularly and slams
Down in the ancient weird tradition of spiking balls after touchdowns.
By now it is so dark that the kids are all flitting darks against the dark.
The ball is brilliant and fluorescent and yellow and gold and amazing.
Maybe these boys are going to play this game until the end of forever.
Maybe they were playing it before the inventor of time invented time.
Maybe the vast fir trees get a huge kick out of watching pass patterns.
Perhaps when the boys finally close up shop because nobody actually
Can see where they are going and a big kid runs down a little kid who
Does his total best not to cry but his brother gets it and calls the game,
Maybe the trees go over the game play by play, savoring the narrative.
Maybe this game is the coolest thing they have seen in three centuries.
Maybe they will talk about that touchdown for another hundred years.
Maybe the whole reason they are here is to keep the rain off the game.
Maybe the kids will be out here tomorrow night and the trees know it.

Mouth to Mouth

A young woman in the last row says to me this morning
Why, yes, I actually *do* know how my grandparents met.
My grampa was a police officer and he dove into a river
To try to save a man who had fallen from a fishing dory,
But the man was underwater too long and didn't make it.
My grandfather tried to resuscitate the man every way he
Knew, mouth-to-mouth and electric wires and everything,
But finally even he had to concede that the man was dead.
He accompanies the body to the hospital in the ambulance
And then he goes home and he changes into a dry uniform
And goes to notify the man's wife that now she is a widow.
So that's how they met, my grandparents. I *love* that story.
My grampa loves to tell that story, and he always finishes
By smiling shy and asking *isn't that how everyone meets?*

At Gnat Creek Hatchery in Clatskanie, Oregon

My sons and I meet a rainbow trout the size of a compact car.
His name is Nick, says the cheerful hatchery manager who is
Sort of talkative because no one ever stops by here too much,
He says, so this is a real Occasion, here's our steelhead pools,
We hatch these fellers and feed 'em up and then let them go to
The creek down there, we raise this gate, see? Yeh, Nick sees
That every year, but he can't go, his mouth is messed up, see?
Some sort of calcium deposit thing that old rainbows get, he's
Figured out how to get an angle on the food we give him, that
Is how he got to be biggern a baseball bat but he wouldn't last
In the wild, be a shame to let him go just to let him starve, eh?
He's probably seven or eight years old. We kind of lost count.
He's been here longern some of the staff. He pals around with
The sturgeon mostly. They live forever, those boys, a hundred
Years maybe. Nick might make it to age twelve or so. He'll be
A monster then, biggern both of you boys. You gents get back
Here in four years or so, just when you're going to college, eh,
And say hey to Nick, he'll be about ready to graduate just then.
Don't tell anybody this because it's not Policy, but a few of us,
The folk who work with Nick, well, when he gets to be twelve,
There'll be one of those little dopey mistakes, someone left the
Pool wall open a little too long and one of the rainbows ran for
The creek, well, that will be Nick. What the hey, his final days,
Let him live large, you know? Probably he'll get eaten for sure,
He's so damn big and he don't know any tricks living out there,
But better he gets eat by a bear than has a heart attack here, eh?

On Crockett Street, in San Antonio, in Texas

My son and I stand and contemplate the heroic ruin of the Alamo
Simmering in the crisp light. Of all the things you could testify to
On this haunted spot, all the wise and piercing things to say about
America and blood and robbery and courage and lines in the dust,
About how small innocent pieces of land with animals and insects
Throbbing on and over and under them get to be shrines if enough
Men die in that dirt, about how history is a story you could tell ten
Different ways a day, one thing that must be said about the Misión
De San Antonio de Valero is that it *gleams* in the morning sunlight.

You have to admit that. I admit this to my boy, forbearing for once
To give him a lecture about greed and grace. After a long pause he
Says, dad, it says here the word Alamo means cottonwood, and that
Tree there is cottonwood, and I bet it's two hundred years old easy,
You wonder if it remembers those days and those guys, you know?
Again I have the terrific urge to inflict a droning lecture on the boy,
To pontificate on the short lives of cottonwoods, and speculate idly
About their gender, these being almost certainly male trees planted
By the state, or the Daughters of the Republic of Texas or someone

Like that, because male cottonwoods don't emit oceans of fluff like
She trees do, but again, for reasons I do not know, I shut my mouth
And we just wander around silently, which we hardly ever get to do.
Usually he is attacking me because he's convinced that I attack him,
And usually I am defending the besieged fortress of general civility,
And there are constant lines drawn in the dirt, and I hate those lines,
Even as I am the one drawing them grimly ten different ways a day.
But not today. Today there's just cottonwood and sun and two guys,
Neither, for once, seething inside the walls of their impregnable forts.

Freshman Ball

Yes, I played high school football. This was in New York.
I was on the freshman team. We dressed in black and gold.
We were the Rams. No one was frightened of us. One time
We lost a game by sixty points. This was on a field of sand
Right by the beach. I didn't like football. I still don't know
Why I played on the football team. I was awful at the game.
I did not like to hit or be hit and I did not like living in mud.
The whole theme of the game seemed to be fighting in mud.
I still remember the day when the names of the starters were
Pinned on the dense window of the gymnasium. There I was,
Starting at linebacker. This was a great surprise. In the game
I just tried to stay out of the way. Many players seemed furious.
There was a lot of cursing. One boy bit another boy's fingers.
Our middle linebacker threw up near the end of the first half.
He had been drinking milk. Players avoided the white puddle.
It was raining. There was a lot of mud. You wouldn't believe
How much mud there was. I couldn't hear or see all that well
Inside my helmet and the mountainous hunch of my padding.
In the second half there came a moment while I was carefully
Sliding away from the play when I noticed the football sitting
Calmly by itself at my feet. I'll always remember the surprise:
Poor thing, all by itself, not being cradled or coddled for once.
It seemed to me that I stood there gaping for quite a long time,
But perhaps it wasn't really that long at all. Memory is a joke,
As you know by now. The other players thrashed and crashed.
I remember that we were not all that far from the white puddle.
Eventually I fell on the ball. Scooping it up and running away

Never occurred to me and even if it had it would have seemed
Awfully dangerous, what with all the players who were angry.
You just wouldn't believe how angry both teams seemed to be.
No one seemed to be enjoying the game, least of all our coach,
Who was stomping his foot on the grass. It was always his left
Foot, I remember that for some reason. How could I remember
That and not remember every word my children have ever said,
Or every caress my wild wife has ever unexpectedly delivered?
But indeed this is the case. We sprinted from the field shouting,
The stalwart defenders, and there was a thin scatter of applause.
It was all downhill from there. The coaches moved me to safety
For everyone's safety. One time I saved a touchdown by poking
The receiver in both eyes as hard as I could. Boy, was *he* angry.
I got good at accidentally tripping receivers, especially tall ones.
We lost that game by sixty. Then the season ended, like a poem.

Pitching in Relief

And as for baseball, I played that curious sport also, for a year,
For any number of poor reasons, one of which was my ejection
From the stalwart Boy Scouts of America, long may they wave,
But suffice it to say that I was, as in freshman football, not deft.
I could not hit, and dove from the batter's box when a curveball
Sliced in, giggling, for a strike; I could not field, and was afraid
Of the ball, no matter what remote position I was inflicted upon,
And of arcane kabbala like the infield fly rule I knew not a thing.
What I did enjoy was the motley wit and snarl of my teammates,
One of whom led a local street gang and carried a brilliant knife,
One of whom would later corner the city market on refrigerators,
And one who became a monk and looks like he will make bishop.
Finally the coach, who I'd guess now was all of twenty years old,
Realized that the only thing I could do that was of a shred of use
To the team was to throw hard, so he made me a pitcher in relief.
I think now he did this from sheer mercy, because he knew there
Would probably never come a time when he'd have to call me in,
But there *did* come such moments, I recall, during which I threw
As hard as I could, and hoped for glory. I could not see the batter
As more than a sort of hazy rectangle, nor could I see the catcher
Very well, but we had an intelligent catcher who learned to shout
At me just before I threw, to give me a general sense of direction,
And so we proceeded on. When the season ended I retired quietly,
Telling only my parents, gentle folks who eloquently said nothing.
But I think now, all these years later, that this dry year of baseball
Was good for me, sculpted me utterly, in that I developed a major
Attentiveness not only to incipient danger, like a ball braining me,

But to all sorts of subtle infinitesimal signals of motion and fervor.
Because I could not see the ball, I watched the players ferociously,
Learning the language of their movement and the reasons they ran.
After a while you didn't have to see the ball to know where it was.
If there was ever a more broadly useful lesson, I do not know of it.

On Contemplating the Heart of the Racehorse Tulloch at a Museum of Such Matters in Melbourne, Australia

Ah, what do I care about horse-racing and its attendant brilliant hoopla,
The whole swirling circus of silks and cash and cups and flimflammish
Blather, furlongs and tiny men with whips and the poor horses thrashed
In circles for the greater good of a populace cheerfully wasting its cash?
So very many carnivals, so much calling of one thing by another name.

But there's something riveting here, and not the fact that this huge heart
Is a third again as big as the usual heart of a horse, or so says the exhibit,
Although you wonder just how many hearts got weighed to discover *that*,
You wonder if there was a guy who was best heartweigher who ever was,
Or a woman who was the genius of their shapes and sizes and ingredients;

And it's deeper than the mere facts of this wild holy creature's existence,
His childhood in the mist of New Zealand, his incredible speed and range,
The puzzling malady that sidelined him for years and almost finished him,
The miraculous medicines that saved him (wine, brandy, and oat porridge),
His quiet death, at age fifteen, in a brilliant paddock, early in the afternoon.

I guess it's the heaviness of hearts, and how we cannot *bear* this heaviness,
But have no choice *but* to bear it and hope for something or somebody who
Will share the load. Isn't it funny that the very thing we all say we hope for,
A heart filled to the brim, a heart at high tide, is exactly the thing we cannot
Bear? Maybe funny isn't the right word. Maybe there are no accurate words.

Maybe words are weak and we waste time trying to make them fill the hole.
Maybe thundering onward with our crammed unbearable hearts is the point.
Maybe Tulloch was a visionary and his heart the relic of a four-legged saint.
Or maybe it's as simple as the kid next to me says: *that heart is way bigger
Than my kid sister's head, and she has a head way bigger than a pumpkin!*

A Prayer for William Morgan of Massachusetts

Story of the day, told by a cheerful young woman at a Quaker college.
After I graduated I went to East Africa on a missionary thing, she says.
Two years, boy, are there ten thousand stories to tell about those years!
I'll tell you just one. For a while we were on a hospital ship off Liberia,
And all kinds of people came out to the ship for all kinds of treatments,
And one morning I was up before first light, and went out to the railing,
And I was standing there just sort of zoning out and staring at the water
When a kid fell off the deck above me, and is falling headlong past me!
Well, I played volleyball in college, and my hands shoot out real quick,
I didn't even have time to think, I was going to *get* to that ball, you bet,
And by unbelievable chance I catch a foot as the kid goes zooming past,
And I haul him in. He's like age four, this kid, you hope he got dropped
By accident, and not given a shove so as to have one less mouth to feed,
But I didn't ask. One of the other girls brought him back to the top deck,
And I just kept thinking, whew, thank God someone invented volleyball,
You know what I mean? The funny thing is that after I got home, I went
And found out who *did* invent the game, a man named William Morgan,
In 1895, in Massachusetts—in the same gym where basketball was born!
To me that's the kind of thing that makes you say your prayers *fervently*.

The Mess of Me

Every day, as you know, one story arrives
And bangs on your head like it was a door.
That story today is about a boy aged seven
On whom so very many sins were inflicted
That he was taken from his murderous clan
And housed in an orphanage for eight years
During which no one ever came to visit him.

He could not bring himself to make a friend,
And no teacher could ever puncture his wall,
So finally the boy decided to commit suicide.
He wrote and signed a note and then stopped.
*I realized that the janitor would have to clean
Up the mess of me, and that did not seem fair,*
He said, in a speech the morning he graduated.

He said this to a crowd of maybe two hundred.
Someone began to clap and then everyone did,
And the man grinning in the rear of the chapel,
I discovered later, was the janitor. I talk to him
Later, the janitor, a quiet and kindly gentleman.
I like when he shares that story, says the janitor,
Because that's *such* a good story about hygiene!

Isn't This France?

Or here's a story. A woman in New Jersey loses her husband
On September 11, it's exactly the phrase she uses, he got lost
That day and never found his way home and to be real honest
I have no idea where he went, she says, so on she goes in life,
I plodded on, she says, or say blundered, wandered, stumbled,
And seven years zoom by, the kids are almost away to college,
When I get a call from a priest friend who says you got to take
This pilgrimage with me to France. I'm thinking what the hell?
I should pay cash to fly to a country where they worship snails?
But he persuades me and I have not been on an honest vacation
Since you know, so no kidding I go with him and his tour gang,
And there's one night we are way out in the country at a chapel,
And they are all inside soaking in the incense and sacred music,
And I sneak outside to get a smoke for like the fourth time since,
And my husband appears to me clear as life on the church walls.
I tell you he was as real as real gets, and he looked damned fine.
I says to him *where are you, love?* and he says *isn't this France?*
This sets us laughing hysterical like two little kids, and we talk
Awhile about some subjects which you do not need to know about,
And then after a while he sort of fades back into the chapel walls.
I can't explain it and haven't the slightest inclination to even try.
It is what it is. All I can say is that I got a great peace that night.
Also the kids and I are going back to France as soon as we can.

Agog

Look, here's what I am trying to say:
The old telephone pole is miraculous.
And the fallen leaves under the roses.
And the molten flow of the old fence
In the schoolyard, and the hedge you
Don't even see until it gets a crewcut.
Everything is the most amazing thing
That ever was in this amazing galaxy,
Period, end of discussion. Questions?

Is Blessed

Listen, says the woman who survived Auschwitz,
I will tell you a story, it's a very mysterious story.
There was a young man in Budapest who figured
Out a way to save some Jews with fake passports,
He saved a lot of Jews, and he told me a little boy
Was the first one he saved, he watched as a guard
On the train stared at the passport and said *alright*,
And the boy he gets on the train, and away it goes.
So the young man he starts to walk away to home,
And clear as a bell he hears a voice say, *is blessed*.
You wouldn't believe how clear this voice speaks,
Says the young man. Wasn't male or female voice.
Just a really clear Voice. Never heard it ever again.
The next time I got somebody safe on the railroads,
I listened real careful when I walked home, but no,
But you can't expecting to be talked to all the time!

Number Ten

At the all-day tournament of freshman high-school teams
I see every kind of player who has ever played basketball:
The geeky kid who is useless but makes one unreal move;
The unbelievable athlete who knows it and that's his flaw;
The big kid who pounds his guy and then is just *indignant*
When he gets called for it; the lightning guard with no off
Hand at all who is terrific the first few minutes and then is
Shut down the rest of the game; the player who yells at his
Teammates when *he* makes a mistake; the guy who is sure
He gets fouled on every play and is theatrical with the refs,
And when he gets the technical he so richly deserves, gets
So upset he earns another; the boy with an acre of baby fat
Who works his ass off and has such clean footwork that he
Just scores and scores and scores without the slightest fuss;
The boy who with arms long as rivers and legs like a heron
Who's got game but is staggered when guys sneeze on him;
The big guy who if he gets to exactly the right spot and gets
The pass delivered at exactly the right instant, hits his hook,
But is otherwise a lumbering slab of confusing adolescence;
The kid who can't miss in warmups but is zero for the game;
The kid who gets plowed into the wall and leaps up snarling
But a moment later after he gets to the bench I notice that he
Is crying quietly. So many stories. The kid who doesn't want
The ball when it arrives, and his patent relief when it is gone;
And my son, the smallest player on the floor but the quickest.
When he checks in to the game I try to only see Number Ten,
Who seems cautious with the ball but wow, what a crossover,

And for all that he's short, he sure inflicts hubbub on defense.
I want him to do well, I want him to be joyous, I want, I want.
But there's nothing I can do now except to love him from afar.

A Boy

Once long ago was swimming through a basketball game
On the hottest drippingest joyousest stickiest mosquitoest
Summernight of that year or maybe the whole millennium
And I drove the baseline hard, locking my elbow on a guy
Just long enough to freeze him a crucial instant and afford
Me room to launch with a slam step and a last hard dribble
And that might have been as high as I ever went in a game,
Man, I was up and away before the guards could sag down,
And there was a delicious second where I was just *floating*,
Until just at the rim two guys hammered me so thoroughly
That I lost the ball, my dense glasses, all sense of direction,
And every shred of the brief conviction I was in command.
At the time I was enraged and I spent the next few minutes
Snarling and barking and sniping at the impassive referees,
But I now think that maybe getting nailed was a subtle gift.
I mean, I kept attacking rims afterwards, every kind of rim,
In every way I could invent—but never with quite the same
Easy assurance that it was my game to do with as I wished.
You can look at this from all sorts of ways, it seems to me.
It sure was a reality check, a package that had to be signed
For sooner or later, and it's sad and funny at the same time
That my peak elevation was followed instantly by a terrific
Crash, but now I think maybe the whole chapter was a gift,
Something that took me years to open and read accurately:
Create with joy, don't get cocky, expect zero from the refs.

On Shotpouch Creek in Oregon

Out back behind the cabin I find a former shrew.
It is, no kidding, the size of a tiny child's thumb.
Hard to believe mammals come so infinitesimal,
Mammals are usually vast epic muscular entities
Not wholly unwilling to dine on us as necessary,
But this tiny miracle, despite modest proportions,
Seems mountainous to me. I mean, its shrewness
Alone is a riveting and mysterious tale, unknown
To my species, for the most part. Are there songs
Among them? Do they conduct tiny symphonies?
Are there dialects by watershed? Are some gentle
And others ferocious? Are there priests and nuns?
Do they have heroic dreams of pummeling bears?
Do they think of this cabin as an alien spacecraft?
The thing to remember is that we don't even know
What we don't even know. That can be frustrating,
Yes, certainly, we all have head-banging moments,
But hey, look at it this way: the galaxy is crammed
With wonders beyond our wildest crazy imagining,
And some of them are the size of your kid's thumb.
Isn't that cool? Isn't that the best thing ever, really?

Mister Wilson

One time a zillion years ago I played on a basketball team
On which eight players had ponytails and our burly center
Had a beard reminiscent of old Walt Whitman or Melville.
We looked like the chorus at a Hassidic hipster convention.
It was funny enough that we all had hair flying in the wind
When we went zooming off on fast breaks, and that Bobby,
Our deft center, looked like U.S. Grant banging the boards,
But the twist was that our coach, Mister Wilson, was Army
Through and through with a buzzcut like a newmown lawn.
He was pained, we could see, that he had to play the freaks,
And he detested the way we played, prone to turnovers and
Essentially wishing only to run like maniacs and try passes
That were not as yet technically possible on this wild earth,
And the poor man would carefully set up intricate play sets,
Sketching them neatly in red and green on his plastic board,
And we would all nod happily, hands on hips, dripping salt,
And then as soon as the whistle blew do whatever we liked
At the highest speed possible. And we did stuff deliberately
To drive him nuts, like call timeout to restore our hairbands
And each game make a ridiculous turnover just to see if we
Could make him make that strangled choking moaning sigh.
At the time we thought we were being cool rebellious guys,
Striking hilarious blows against The Man and his discipline,
His regimentation, his greedy demand for order and pattern,
But now I think we were maybe meaner than we ever knew.
We were just teenagers, heedless and selfish, all too normal,
You have to be an idiot before you can desist being an idiot,

But now I see Mister Wilson, fedora hat surfing his crewcut,
Always wearing a suit even when running practice sessions,
That pained wince on his face as we deliberately threw wild,
And I get a sense of what made him wince: all that graceful
Athleticism, all that sweet energy, all that possible creativity,
All that wild juice that, bottled, might have made great wine.
I guess he was all of forty then, old Mister Wilson, and three
Days a week he left his wife and kids and house and gave us
What he had, and we threw it away, laughing. The best thing
About turnovers, though, is that you always get the ball back.

The Arrow of Light

Not to mention my tumultuous experiences as a Cub Scout,
From the first den meeting in the Lutheran minister's home
Under epic elm trees that loomed over the house like angels
To the labyrinthine tasks required to rise from Wolf to Bear,
Or, unthinkably, unattainable by mortal boys, the legendary
Arrow of Light. It was said that one boy ever from our town
Had earned this, and it was *stitched to the skin on his chest*,
And it had saved him from bullets, and being nailed by cars,
And one time the Arrow had even conspired to derail a train
That was about to crush him, although it did mangle his bike.
The older brother of a Bobcat had not only seen but *touched*
The bicycle, and lived, although he got a huge electric shock,
Or so said the Bobcat—we were not sure he was trustworthy,
As he was Lutheran, and so not one of the elect and/or saved.
Plus he was stuck at Bobcat as all the other guys rose to Bear,
Even me, a lad who later in life stalled at Scout Second Class.
I cannot now remember the tasks that earned us advancement,
I have vague memories of misadventures with plaster of Paris
And whittling knives and doggedly trailing cats through snow
Knowing beyond doubt that they absolutely were tiny cougars,
And whispering to each other about the amazing grim courage
Of the kid who had the Arrow of Light patch sewn on his skin.
The Bobcat said his brother was careful not to let just *anybody*
See it, but that *he* could see it just about any time he wanted to,
And one boy, a Wolf who clearly was right at the edge of Bear,
Said he would pay a *dollar* to see the Arrow, there was no *way*
That was for real, but the Bobcat said, with pride, he would not
Participate in such dealings, as that was not the Cub Scout Way.
My estimate of Lutheranism, previously low, rose immediately.

A Sudden Episcopalian

And the first real job I ever had, other than flinging newspapers
And sprinting away sobbing with fear from gangs of murderous
And slavering dogs, two of which had actually eaten a paperboy
Leaving nothing but his ghostly sneakers and lonely belt buckle,
And another of which was reputed to be the *capo* of all the dogs
On the whole south shore of the island, running all sorts of scam
Up to and including some shady dealings with the Episcopalians,
Was washing a procession of pots and pans in the village bakery.
You wouldn't believe how very many pots and pans a baker uses.
I bet there were a thousand easy, some of them bigger than Idaho.
There were three pots in particular that were so big I had to climb
Into them to clean them properly and I couldn't see over the edge.
More than once the baker would say goodnight and close up shop
And I didn't hear him, being deep in the echoing country of a pot,
Pondering the dogs and their various deals with the Episcopalians.
What *didn't* they have their paws in? The trouble with conspiracy
Is that you always see more than really exists, that's the brilliance
Of it, the shiver of trepidation, the shard of expectation that a dog
Is in the next alley, hunched insouciantly, two grim Episcopalians
Ready to do his nefarious bidding. I quit the bakery job soon after,
Partly because the walk home after emerging startled from the pot
Was just too much for me. I kept expecting a sudden Episcopalian,
And that's no way to live a life. Soon after that I got a job in a beer
Store, in a sunnier section of town, and started going to Mass daily,
Just in case, and gave the paper route to a brother—yet another sin.

99

The Bris

Whereas the first time I met Judaism face to face
Was being dragooned into a *bris* at age seventeen,
At which some poor sniveling infant, whose name
I did not even know, was relieved of a flap of skin
In his crucial nether masculine parts by an ancient
Rabbi who didn't see well and seemed to be using
A butter knife. I was there on totally false pretense,
Shanghaied because I looked Jewish, and I prayed
For anonymity, which He saw fit to grant unto me.
I kept a hawk eye on the other nine men to be sure
To do what they did, but mostly what they did was
Look confused, something I was already masterful
At without the slightest effort or any training at all.
So the ceremony trundled along. It was late spring.
The rabbi flourished his butter knife like Abraham.
I remember that the light glinted off his eyeglasses.
There were murmurs but maybe that was the radio.
The kid was the color of rust and duff and sawdust.
I felt bad for the kid. He looked like a sweet potato.
He was staring at the rabbi's shining spectacles too.
Outside I could hear the bird tribes arguing bitterly.
I remember that the kid was about as big as a crow.
The other men were all wearing a sort of tablecloth.
I remember realizing that Yeshua the son of Joseph
Must have been in just this remarkable predicament.
I remember my immense relief when it was all over
And I could escape without being fingered as a goy.

All these years later I can see the rabbi's eyeglasses
And his impatient knife. Could it be that everything
That ever happened is still waiting to happen again?

Death of a Novelist

In his living room, on a June afternoon, in rural Minnesota,
While folding the laundry. Lived alone in a college cottage.
The college was Benedictine. *Ora et labora*, prayer & work.
He had taught there many years. Students thought him testy
But excellent. There is hardly any laundry when you are 82
Years old, almost. Almost every day he walked to the grave
Of his wife and daughter, gone ahead. Seven pairs of socks,
He had discovered, cover about every situation and weather.
And what man in his right mind really needs more than four
Pairs of pants? Two pairs of black for weddings and wakes,
Brown for daily use, white in memory of Betty, who always
Loved to dress for summer, and itched to buy him a summer
Suit. Why did I not let her? Why my insistence on frugality?
We did have the four other children. Such very little money.
A National Book Award doesn't pay for all that many socks.
She would always say, Betty would, maybe you didn't need
Many clothes when you were in prison for refusing the draft,
Jim, but our children are not prisoners, and I *like* to dress up
For summer. He folds the towels first, to get his hands loose.
For years after their daughter died he washed and folded her
Clothes too. Finally he quit. Those years we lived in Ireland,
He thinks, my God, how did we manage that army of socks?
I don't remember now. *She'd* know. He folds his underlings,
As his daughters used to call what he called unmentionables,
A word he heard from his own father, who heard it from his,
And so on: stories ripple and wander just like that, he thinks.
I spent my whole life on rivers of stories. And folding socks.

Ora et labora. Stabbing pains in upper chest. Novelist James Farl Powers, age 81, died on Saturday afternoon in his home. He is survived by four children and an amazing pile of socks.

    —in memory of J.F. Powers, 1917–1999

Her

Twice in recent weeks I have found people I love praying
On their knees in their pajamas in the middle of the night,
Praying so hard that neither of them saw or heard me fade
Away silently to go pray myself, under the blessed covers.
You wonder if what you say soaks into the soils and souls
Of your kids, you are fairly sure it doesn't, given the daily
Evidence to the contrary, but then suddenly there's a child
On his knees by his bed, and everything slides everywhere
Inside your skin. A minute ago you were telling them they
Could approach Herself at any time with any complication
Imaginable, because you know all too well She is attentive,
And then they run sprinting away from any hint of religion
Or belief or trust or spiritual search, and even as you loudly
Proclaim, mostly to convince yourself, that this is a healthy
Thing, you hope, deep in your bones, that they will find Her.
To see their mother in the dining room on her lovely knees,
In the brilliant river of the moon, as the cedar prays outside,
I can't say that's a surprise, you never met a mom who digs
The Mother more than *that* mom, but to find our son bowed
In prayer, his fists clenched, asking for help with every iota
Of his being . . . I don't have any words that carry real weight.
All I can do is tell you about it and somehow that's a prayer
Too, you know what I mean? Every story matters more than
We know, or we ever will know—but at least we know *that*.

September 11, 2009

Sat by the river for a long time making sure it was still working.
There's a pile of finches in the currants stuffing themselves silly.
This one finch slurped so many berries he could hardly get aloft.
He sort of lurched off the branch and lumbered into the holy air.
It seemed like the other finches were razzing him but maybe not.
He fell toward the river like a huge currant covered with feathers.
You have to grin at the greedy green thrilled persistence of it all,
You know what I mean? Because there are finches in the bushes,
Exactly so. What could ever be a more eloquent prayer than that?

The Sparrow

Or, hey, listen, *here's* a story for you.
A friend of mine who is 96 years old
And blind but still living in her beach
Cabin hears her cat capture a sparrow
Which the cat then presents as a prize.
My friend cradles the bird in a sponge
And goes to the front door and throws
Out the sponge, and then goes to wash
The dishes, only to realize she's using
The sparrow, who objects strenuously.
Now, this is a terrific story from every
Angle imaginable: deft murderous cat,
Sparrow who didn't die, lady giggling,
The grin that just opened on your face,
The child who will fall down laughing
Later when you say now *here's* a story . . .

Quid Hoc Ad Aeternitatem

Quid hoc ad aeternitatem, as old Saint Bernard of Clairvaux
Used to mumble when faced with the usual parade of travail,
What does it matter in the light of eternity? And yet, and yet,
With total respect for eternity, don't you love your problems,
The smallness of them, the salt and roar of them, considering
The alternative? The blizzards of bills I can never pay in toto,
The surly son, the dismissive daughter, the wet shabby house,
The battered car, the shivering pains, the grim brooding debts,
The dark thread of fear that I might not have been a good dad,
The feeling sometimes that maybe there was a better husband
For my wife if only she had hung in the contest a little longer,
And the ones that haunt me every minute of the blessed week,
The health and joy of our kids, and the fragility of their future;
But there are great moments when I realize that all the muddle
Is so very much better than aeternitatem. Could it be that what
Keeps us awake at night are the greatest gifts we can ever get?
Just thinking. Because soon enough, as real time is accounted,
We'll be muttering Latin with Bernard, and what we will want
More than anything, even there, in the incomprehensible Light,
Is to be in a chair late at night, frightened, rocking a sick child.

Her Hands on the Shoulder of My Coat

I am pretty sure but not totally sure that Mass in this town is at eleven,
So I shamble across the street from the motel and arrive neurotic early,
I hate to slide into Mass late and croak the door and get the death stare
From the old ladies, what *is* it about a head scarf that makes you mean,
And I wait for the crowd but only six people wander in and one leaves,
A man with a huge cowboy hat who kisses a woman and then basically
Runs down the aisle grinning, what in heaven's name is the story *there*,
But just then the lanky priest emerges and says *in nomine Patris et Filii*
Et Spiritus Sancti, and I realize this is a Latin Mass—the old Tridentine
Rite in which I was soaked as a boy. The old tongue is a physical shock.
I can feel the language like my mom's hands on the shoulder of my coat.
For an instant that no instrument will ever measure I am in the pew with
My dad sitting by the aisle because he will soon help with the collection,
And my three brothers, the oldest surly and tall and handsome and bored,
And my wry wild lone sister who will incredibly someday become a nun,
And my mom, in the pew behind us because Mass was so crowded today,
Her hands on the shoulder of my coat. Maybe they were there to keep me
From punching a younger brother, or maybe she was slipping me a dollar,
Or perhaps we tell each other that we love each other without words more
Easily than we do with words. *Sanctus, Sanctus, Sanctus.* I bet you a buck
My mom was sitting in the pew behind us because none of us kids wanted
To sit closer and make room for her, we were all our own selfish republics
Then, adamant about what the world owed us. *Nobis quoque peccatoribus.*
The tall priest this morning sings occasionally but I long ago lost my Latin.
Domine non sum dignus—well, that line I know too well: I am not worthy.
And *ite missa est*, the last words, the Mass is over. The other five attendees
Genuflect and vanish but I sit there a long while with her hands on my coat.

My brothers jostle for space and one nearly crushes my dad's hat. My sister
Is the only one of us who turns to see where mom is. My dad gives us coins.
Eventually the thin priest leans out of the sacristy and gives me the fish eye.
I hope to find my mom waiting outside the church but when I open the door
The first thing I see is the guy with the cowboy hat kissing the woman again,
Which feels like exactly the right thing at exactly the right moment, as usual.

A Shrew

One time a long time ago when I was supple and strong and rubbery
As a snake in a hurry I was on my belly in the bush and saw a shrew
In the litter of leaves and for the longest shortest moment we startled
Each other considerable but maybe the scale of our encounter was so
Ludicrously unbalanced that our normal fear of weird missed the bus,
Leaving us eye to eye under the epic ambition of a huckleberry tangle.
I remember thinking that the shrew was awfully near my two absolute
Favorite eyeballs and that shrews are said to be terrors among the tiny.
I remember that it was the size of a thumb or a thimble or a little cigar.
I remember that it had a lustrous dense shining coat as black as can be.
I remember wondering even then what it could possibly be wondering.
I remember that he or she seemed to be missing a northeast appendage.
Many questions and angles of inquiry presented themselves to me later,
Such as what combination of factors could deduct a limb from a shrew,
And what manner of beast could have executed said deletion—perhaps
A romantic tangle, a political wrangle, a religious debate turned savage
As so often has been the case? Or the usual suspects snuffling for meat.
Or maybe shrews, who do not live long in the way the world calculates,
Dissolve a leg at a time, growing ever closer to the sensuous roil of soil,
As do we all. But meanwhile there's such a hungry immediacy, correct?
All these years later that's what I remember from that shrewish moment,
That I stopped thinking and just stared. Yes, partly because I was scared,
But there was something beyond curiosity or the startle of astonishment.
For just an instant I paid attention with every shard and iota of my being.
Maybe we couldn't survive if we were like that all the time, I know that,
But when it happens we see that which none of us can find the words for.
Sometimes we are starving to see every bit of what is right in front of us.

Death of a Maple

Proof number fifty thousand that there are no small stories,
Only vast gaps in our perceptive nets for revelatory stories:
A monumental old maple tree on campus suddenly cleaves
Itself one afternoon, no ostensible reason, no rain, no wind,
Half of it just sheers off with an epic rending moaning sigh,
And soon thereafter two quiet chain-smoking tree surgeons
Appear and slowly calmly efficiently slice up the fallen tree,
And then slowly lop the rest of the creature leaving a stump
They sculpt into a redolent shimmering rooted wooden pew.
They disappear every scrap and curl of shaving and sawdust,
And I watch as a puzzled squirrel wanders around the bench.
It's the not-thereness of the maple that's the most astounding
Thing, you know what I mean? The light bends in new ways,
The plants and animals are startled, people walking by pause
Confused but not knowing quite what's changed in the scene.
You can get absorbed completely just by the surgeons' skills,
Or by what must have been a century of memory and witness
In whatever tongue and consciousness maple trees are issued,
Or by the painful comedy of the completely confused squirrel,
But what gets to me as I watch the squirrel explore cautiously
Is the thorough, inarguable absence of what was so adamantly
Present. The light bends in new ways. There's a hole in the air.
You flutter your hands where there used to be a living creature.
You can *say* as long as you remember and tell stories it's alive,
But it *isn't* alive, and no one knows what happened to anything
Other than the skeleton which ended up as firewood and a pew.
I guess in the end we either believe what was alive is still alive,
In ways that we will never be able to understand, or we believe
In the persistent production of extraordinary pews. You choose.

Chalikor

Kid steps out of the crowd at the ceremony and receives his bronze star
For bravery in action against enemy forces with disregard for his safety,
And then steps back into the burble and essentially vanishes. I seek him
Out afterward. He is standing under a cedar tree smoking. He looks like
He's twenty years old but really he is thirty odd, he says, accent on odd.
It was in the Chalikor Valley in Afghanistan, man. The Chalikor Valley,
There's a name I won't forget. Jumped by Taliban, fight was nine hours,
I did my job. I am honored by the medal, absolutely, but basically every
Guy there earned a medal. Chalikor, just the sound of it is spooky, right?
Chalikor, won't hear *that* word the rest of my life without weapon check.
He finishes his cigarette. He looks like he's about twenty years old, max.
He even has one of those tiny beatnik third-armpit attempts at chin music.
He's a student now at the university. Studying history. Sophomore. Love
That word, *sophomore*, he says, it sounds cool, like *girls* and *sandwiches*.
History major. Wants to be a teacher. I'd teach my kids to miss Chalikor,
Man, he says, smiling. I'd teach them to settle disputes with chess pieces,
You know what I'm saying? Teach them bronze stars are what used to be.

An Afternoon with C. P. Cavafy

Or Konstantinos, as he said quietly after a while, a little shy,
Let us call each other the words our mothers gave us to wear.
We were in the sun among dense burly rhododendron bushes.
How could that be, you will say, Cavafy is eighty years dead,
And I cannot answer your excellent question. There he stood,
Though, a slight man, well-dressed, not wealthy but attentive
To his appearance, I would say. It was unusually cold and we
Both angled ourselves to get all the sun possible. Now I wish,
He said, that I had spent more time on the thingness of things,
And less perhaps on the resonant echo of the past in daily life;
It's the moment that is the great thing, not understanding how
The moment has arrived at the tail of an incredible procession.
Oh yes, I said, the treeness of trees, the crowness of the crows,
You could spend a thousand lifetimes just on eyeballs, or dust.
Maybe we do. Maybe this moment begins a whole new parade.
I didn't want to make time stop, he said gently. It was a prayer,
Really, a way to salute, to say thank you but not to Personages;
Do you know what I mean? O yes, sir, I said. I have concluded
That what I am to do is generally offer thanks, using ink marks.
Exactly so! he says, exactly so! There are so wonderfully many
Witnesses, yes? Of whom so very many are poets without pens;
Those are the ones I would celebrate, if I was again given voice.
But perhaps now my work is to be your sudden impulse, or lens.

Steak Knives: A Note

On the day my wife married me, a wry friend, later a priest,
Gave us a set of knives for the kitchen, six of them for steak.
Someone else gave us steak knives also, I disremember who.
In toto then we may assume that at the outset there were ten.
Someone then gave us three children and the array of knives
Suffered terribly. Two broke while being used for absolutely
The wrong reasons. It is *not* important that you know how to
Whip knives end over end into a thin tree from twenty paces,
No matter what your brother says or how cool the movie was.
Another knife helped balance the parakeet. I'll explain about
That some other time. Suffice it to say that birds are neurotic.
Occasionally I have found a steak knife under a boy's pillow,
The child explaining that there are a lot of bad guys out there,
Which is not something I can deny, although I took the knife.
I have found steak knives in the bathroom and in the laundry.
I have found them being used as screwdrivers and doorstops.
Several other of the knives vanished quietly over the decades,
Perhaps leaving, one by one, by prearranged codes or signals.
Perhaps the multiple sisters of my beloved have been stuffing
Our steak knives into their voluminous purses for many years.
This is unlikely although they have purses bigger than Illinois.
You wonder why it is that women slog such bulging suitcases
Around their daily labors—do they really require all that stuff,
Or do they need to be prepared for flight, like, say, a parakeet?
But back to the knives. I used to bark about their evanescence,
Snarl and whimper and yip and generally be a grouch about it,
But now I think it's kind of cool, it shows the passage of years

In the house, that we used so many knives for so many reasons
Good and bad, that we were given each other, granted a family,
Slathered with tumultuous and difficult and hilarious blessings
In more ways than we will ever be able to account. It turns out
That grace is a steak knife; a wonderfully sharp gift, for a time.

On a Hill in New York in Summer
as My Cousin Enters the Convent

This is my sweetest gentlest grinningest funniest wittiest cousin Maureen,
And someone among the gathered sweating camera-snappy ancient adults
Murmurs *hey you know what no one's saying is* what *a loss for some guy,*
But no one takes it up and every adult is riven, one way or another, as she
Takes her place, dressed in all blinding searing frightening antarctic white.
It is the hottest day in history. There are vast hordes and armies of cicadas.
We kids are not paying much attention. There are sudden savage fistfights.
The general feeling among the kids is that this is a kind of disguised Mass,
And so our forced attendance is totally unfair, though we all like Maureen.
The general feeling among the kids is that we will never ever see her again.
Probably she will be assigned to the laundry and never see the light of day.
The mother superior murmurs something sonorously about *bride of Christ,*
Which is a weird idea no matter how you cut it, mutters one of my cousins,
Plus if she married a Jewish guy, mom would have a fit right here and now.
You wouldn't believe how many cicadas were thrilling all at the same time.
You never heard so many blessed insects insisting on something all at once.
Just before she entered the gate into the huge convent she spun and grinned
Her huge grin at us like an arrow or a rocket. She had a grin like a high tide.
Her grin hauled up your grin like a fish no matter how disgruntled you were.
It was interesting to see the adults teeter between pride and a sort of sadness.
One of my brothers found the mother lode of sweetgum burrs and he started
A vast and epic battle that swayed up and down the hill by the convent walls.
We got so absorbed in the battle that we missed the actual moment when she
Vanished into the rest of her life, which there wasn't all that much more of it.
She died young. So we were correct that we would never get to see her again.
But some things always are, no matter how long ago they were. Like how she

Spun suddenly and beamed at us and spun back so fast hardly anyone noticed. Her grin could totally kick the butt of any other grin you might possibly name. If there was a hall of fame for grins which there should be she's in, first ballot. We all milled around. The cicadas kept roaring. Perhaps there was a reception. Her grin was going roughly southeast and we think eventually it hit Argentina.

First Swimming Lesson, East Bathhouse, Jones Beach, July 1964

There were a lot of us and we all had thin pale peeled legs like leeks.
The water was brilliant and shimmering and alluring and transparent.
It seemed like such a shame to insert ourselves in such a lovely thing.
We were all shivering. It was early in the morning. The shy lifeguard
Called us tadpoles. The flags on the vaulting walls snapped like rifles.
Our suits were too tight and we worried people could see . . . you know.
My brother stood next to me. He was the skinniest kid who ever lived.
Most of him was feet. His arms were so long he could touch Missouri.
Why is it that we remember some things that don't seem to be crucial,
Like a crisp rippling morning at the pool many years ago, and we lose
Other moments that you might think mountainous, like sex and death?
Maybe our memories are a lot smarter than we are. Maybe my brother,
And his frightened smile, and the lawn of his hair, and the huge knobs
Of his knees like bulbs on a bush, maybe those memories matter most.
Maybe if I forget that he reached for my hand just before we leaped in,
Reached for it without a thought, reached for me because he needed to,
Because he loved me and I loved him in ways that we can never gauge,
Then he would never have reached for my hand that glittering morning,
And we would all be terribly reduced; not just him and me, but you too.

The Song That Ena Zizi Sang

As usual one story will have to serve for one million stories.
That is the way of stories. You might think that a lone story
Cannot possibly do that, and you would be right and wrong.
So here is Ena Zizi. She is seventy years old. The house fell
Down on her when an earthquake hammered Port-au-Prince.
She was there in the dark for a week, her leg and hip broken.
In the beginning she talked to a man who was buried nearby.
He was a priest, he said. After two days he fell silent so Ena
Talked only to God, she said. After a week, she was rescued
By a team called the Gophers. They slid her out on plywood.
Ena sang all the way out of the rubble: she had begun to sing
When she heard the scrabbling of the Mexicans' search dogs.
No one can remember if there were any words in the singing,
But everyone remembers the lady singing. Ena says she does
Not remember what song she was singing. I was *very* thirsty,
She says. I sang and sang. Everyone there wept, and clapped,
And they went back to work. But Ena is still singing the song.
That's what I wanted to tell you. You can't not hear her song.
I think perhaps that's a song that once it gets born never ends.
I think maybe there are more songs floating than we can hear.
I think we all know that and we all get a little tired and forget.
But look, there's Ena rising from the dead again, and singing!

On Watching Patsy Cline Sing during
Her Last Television Appearance, 1963

There's a moment about halfway through the song
When she just lets the microphone sag to her waist
But her voice gets even *more* deep and big and sad;
How could that be? I watch over and over and over.
You can't say anything casual about Americanness,
It's a huge idea stuffed with blood and comedy and
Rivers and ketchup and cougars and lies and trucks,
But some things point toward what it means, a little.
Like Patsy. She changed her name—how American
Is that? And was by every account a funny and kind
Soul, quietly paying friends' rents, that sort of thing.
She jotted her will on airplane stationery. Somehow
That's Americanness, doing something important in
An airy and informal way. *O I sing like I hurt inside,*
She said to a disc jockey who asked about her "style."
Like all moms she didn't think she was good enough
As a mom although her kids did. Recording her final
Record she cried through most of the yearning music;
You can hear her sob when she sings about her lover.
She called everyone Hoss, male and female. She said
Her mom was her very best friend. She finally forced
Her way out of cowgirl outfits, into ballroom dresses,
Because I want to dress like I always wanted to dress,
She said—Americans get to create themselves, finally.
She had "feelings" about her death months beforehand.
We are a morbid and death-haunted people absolutely.

Her last gig was a benefit, for a friend who died poor.
You never met a more generous tribe than Americans.
Her airplane went down in a storm, deep in the woods.
The forests primeval which we still praise and murder.
Entrepreneurs rushed to the crash site to scavenge bits
And pieces of her things, her cigarette lighter, slippers,
Wristwatch, her belt studded with her rhinestone name.
We do love glitter and violence and the shiny deceased.
She is buried in her native Virginia and there is a tower
That plays hymns every evening at six. We love to pray.
She died young, barely thirty. On television she finishes
The song without the slightest flourish or flash or crash.
She just ends with effortless grace and slides off smiling.
There have been so many wonders, so many remarkable
Generosities here. Maybe we just don't say that enough.

On Preferring the Older Rosemary Clooney to Her Younger, More Famous Incarnation

I suppose mostly it's the voice, much deeper and grainier,
Even a little breathless in her last songs, you quietly hope
She'll be able to swing that note up and away at the finish,
But it's the inarguable hint of gentle amusement there, too.
Perhaps endurance is a greenhouse for patience and mercy.
Not to mention she had five kids and was a legendary aunt.
If her life was a flash series of newspaper photographs you
Would see the girl singer *the best in the business* says Bing
Crosby, and the movie star, and the epicenter of the tabloid
World when she eloped, and the press conference when she
Broke down and sobbed the whole hour, and her quiet thrill
As a superb jazz singer at the end *I can even pick the songs*,
She said, *no one ever asked me that before* but we wouldn't
See the night their father left the house with all their money
And never returned and Rosie, age seventeen, and her sister
Betty are living alone with no phone or heat collecting soda
Bottles to get money to eat, or the million hours she cradled
Her five kids in five years, imagine the mountain of diapers,
Or how years after her divorce, the kids all grown and away,
She's at a stoplight and looks over and sees a man she loved
Many years before and he sees her and she yells her number,
Didn't think a bit, she said, *my voice just came jumping out*,
And she peels away in embarrassment but he writes it down,
With his finger in the dust on his dashboard, and they marry,
And all through the last years when I love her voice the best
She'd go home after singing to a guy who liked to cook soup.

Imagine Rosie walking into that thicket of scent and smiling.
That's the final photograph in the series, say—she's seventy,
Weary from recording all day, but she walks into the kitchen
And there's her husband grinning and stirring. Lots of letters,
Rosie, he says. You sit, and I will bring in the best soup *ever*.

Near Fig Tree Road, in Sydney, Australia

Once upon a time I was at dinner with a lean priest named Michael.
This was on a long muscle of soil called Hunters Hill by the harbor.
There was a Catholic school nearby in a sprawling field and around
The field were Mark and John and Paul and James and Mary streets.
What, no Luke and Matthew? I asked. He grinned. Jupiter and Mars
Streets are south a bit, he said. We like to cover all the bases, as you
Say in your country. And aptly our broadest street here is Augustine.
Wondrous lesson, that man, but he has been imprisoned by theology.
Grant me chastity but not yet, everyone knows that hilarious remark,
But we perhaps do not remember that he was African, and had a son,
And a steady girlfriend for many years before his epiphanic moment,
Which occurred under a fig tree not unlike, perhaps, one of our trees.
You will remember that Gautama also achieved light under a fig tree.
So one lesson we could draw for the church today would be more fig
Trees on general principles, a fig being perhaps the very tree of Eden.
The Prophet Mohammed, God bless him and grant him peace, dearly
Loved figs, and they are mentioned everywhere in his Book and ours.
Now, we might draw the lesson from Augustine that all bishops must
Have a child and a steady girlfriend as a first education in God's love,
But that is . . . unlikely, in my lifetime and probably yours, so I suggest
We begin with figs, which would not only foment epiphany, but offer
Meanwhile a most delicious fruit. Should we ask for a plate of them?

Icarus Enters His First High School Baseball Game

Eighth inning: he trots out to right field. He has been warming up
The right fielder during inning breaks but now they switch places
With a little casual fist bump as they trot past. My heart hammers.
His throws are insouciant but he fiddles his cap one million times.
I don't know whether to hope he gets some balls hit to him or not.
He doesn't shade toward the line for a lefty and I want to yell hey
But he's on his own; he wants that more than anything these days.
He's made that abundantly vulgarly spectacularly sneeringly clear.
He vaguely backs up first and second on infield plays and vaguely
Drifts into cutoff position on a deep shot to center. Then a looping
Ball deep to right: he takes two steps in and then retreats hurriedly
And the ball drops behind him but he grabs it and whips a startling
Rope to second to hold the runner. His teammates yell *good throw!*
He does not smile. The way the late light catches his face makes it
Hard for me to breathe. Tomorrow we will roar at each other again.
The inning ends with a blessedly straightforward grounder to short.
On the way home I am sure he will be rude. Perhaps this is heaven.

Sister Anne Marie

It was in second grade that I discovered I could not see.
This thought had never occurred to me in all my years.
When Sister Anne spun suddenly to write on the board,
Her rosary big as a halter desperately trying to catch up
With a clack and clatter like railroad cars, I leaned over
To one or the other of the kids near me to read what we
Were supposed to know. Isn't that why God made rows
Of desks, so you had good sight angles in all directions?
But she noticed, did Sister Anne. She noticed each of us.
She was probably all of twenty. We thought her ancient.
But she knew which boy could not read, not even a little,
And which of us didn't actually forget lunch, and who is
Wearing his older sister's winter coat with the lapels cut.
She sent me to the nurse one time, perhaps I had a fever,
But the note she wrote said check his eyes. Yes, I read it.
The nurse put it on the corner of her desk and I peered at
It later, worried I was being sent to Siberia or something.
But that finished with me getting glasses, which changed
Everything. The universe had edges! I never did recover.
Imagine what it was like to put on spectacles, for the first
Time, after never seeing the clarity and geometry of it all.
Imagine the jolt of absolute stunned delight. Imagine *that*,
Just for a minute. All these years later I can't stop smiling.

The Squirrel

Here you go. Here's a moment to ponder carefully.
We think that there are greater and lesser moments
But how immensely and ridiculously wrong this is.
For here is a boy riding along the street in summer.
He is perhaps six years old. His bike is wildly blue.
He sees a smear of squirrel in the street. He pauses,
Using the heels of his sneakers as brakes. He looks,
He dismounts, he sets his kickstand, he looks down.
He kneels and gathers up the shredded creature and
Walks to the shady ravine where we saw the coyote
That time and he gives the squirrel to the tiny creek.
He washes in a muddy puddle and then he rides off.
I am the man who saw and testifieth of these things,
And what I say is true. I saw a boy bow before holy
Things, for all things are holy, and he reminded me,
And so now I remind you. Go thou and do likewise.

Easter

Windy, same as usual. Shivering daffodils, huddled crocuses.
Sunbursts that are essentially a dark joke. Spattering of moist
Proto-hail, says our sister, who will eventually become a nun.
Funny that we remember single words spoken forty years ago.
The huddle of shoulders in pews, the hands held out for Hosts.
The rich russet scent of raincoats and overcoats and umbrellas.
The slight polite hesitation as someone looks to lift the kneeler.
The way everyone kneels except the very old and the surgicals.
The clasps pinning down mantillas and veils and white scarves.
The burly theater of it all, the ancient tidal rise and fall and ebb
And startling resurrection against all sense and patent evidence.
The awful genius of the faith is that it is so much more and less
Than religion; we have no choice but to insist on a resurrection,
And choose one among us to drag a cross, and then leap from it
And emigrate, but not before collecting documentary witnesses;
Otherwise we are all merely walking compost, and where is the
Fun in that, not to mention why not commit crimes twice daily?
And at the other end of the spectrum, not one soul on that rainy
Easter morning long ago cared a whit about theological matters.
They did not even care if the thin man once died and rose again.
They were there, in clans and tribes and couples, for each other,
Out of respect and affection, and habit and custom, and because
They wanted to give their children a thing they couldn't explain
Very easily, something to run away from and later back towards,
Something insistent that didn't make sense then and still doesn't.
Something you can easily disprove and can never actually prove,
Which is basically the point. We cover it with smoke and money,

With vestments and learned commentary, with visions and edicts,
But under the cloth there is only wild hope, to which we give His
Face, sitting there by the lake quietly eating baked fish and bread.
At the end of the meal we walked out into the rain, singing badly.

Poem for the Four Goslings Killed by the Dog Today

It's his nature. It's what he was trained to do over millions of years.
It's probably how he survived when he lived in the woods for years.
Someone abandoned him and he was lost and you could see his ribs
Like huge knobby fingers. Now, after the four deaths, he is uneasily
Sprawled by the door. He knows something is different in the house.
Their crime was to be alluring and available. I murmur explanations.
The parents are in the pool by the retention dam. The quartet of limp
Bodies we left in the woods. Something will eat them. Two goslings
Died immediately and one lived a moment longer and one, saved by
The boy who jumped into the thornbushes after the dog, died slowly.
These things happen. A door left ajar. But the children move silently
The rest of the day. All the lives that never got much chance to open.
The kids are shocked, but maybe this is the best thing I could never see
A way to teach them in a way they wouldn't forget. This isn't papers
Due for school. It's babies with bloody holes and snapped necks and
Parents so weary and empty that perhaps the coyotes will catch them
Tonight. Death ripples on and on. We hardly admit this. It just sleeps
A little and then goes back to work. You can see why we made a god
Of it, relentless and inarguable. We finish mowing the lawn. A goose
Pair, if their first nesting is unsuccessful, may raise a second brood in
The same reproductive season. *What is it I should teach my children?*
That life is irrepressible? But their lives are not. There are many dogs
Of every shape and size. That death is relentless? Yet here we all are,
On the most brilliant of afternoons, not dead. The dog should be dead,
All things considered; how a young hound could survive in the woods
Is a mystery—but he lived. My boy washes off blood from the thorns.

The Thirty

One time I was sitting on a high hill in Australia,
This was a year when my marriage was teetering,
And a priest strolled out of the nearby monastery
And sat down companionably on the cedar bench
And didn't say anything, for which I was grateful
Beyond words. Parrots rocketed by and a possum
Scrabbled in a pine tree. The brush-tailed possum,
Said the priest finally, while dedicated to its mate,
Devotes a good part of its time to solitary pursuits,
The speculation among scientists being that this is
Healthy for both partners, who come to each other
With fresh information, as it were. I didn't answer
Him directly and he didn't press the point, and our
Talk turned to rugby and oysters, and off we went,
Each to his own pursuits; I never forgot that bench,
Though. For every greedy evil rapacious liar priest
I think maybe there are thirty great and subtle men.
We forget this. Certainly we should dangle a rapist
From the pine tree by his nuts, but those other men,
The men who know what not to say, who hand you
Their ears without cash or expectations or religious
Claptrap, who spend their days as patient witnesses,
Who bend their time to singing the holiness of it all,
Who wake up before dawn and don their priesthood
Willingly like a thorny endlessly tumultuous prayer,
Those are the thirty this poem turned out to be about.

The Sea

We were perhaps eight and ten, my brother
And I, both invited to a house by the ocean,
And that first night, after lots of hullabaloo,
We were ladled into old summer camp cots
That hadn't been used since Lincoln's time,
And I remember, as if it was just last week,
That we both felt something grim in the sea
For the first time—a cold careless mastery,
Maybe. I still can't articulate this very well.
We lay there listening to the infinitesimally
Tiny increase in wavelet volume as the tide
Came in rustling acres of mussel shells and
Old boats and horseshoe crabs and the pots
That jailed uncountable families of lobsters,
And the *scents* sliding through the windows
Were loud, dense, lurid, something to smell
Gingerly and back away from. I was scared
More than I would ever admit to my brother.
We had been to the beach two million times,
Sure, but those were brilliant days, an ocean
To taunt, not one that smelled like all deaths
That ever were, marinated for a billion years
And then sent smiling into canals and inlets.
Low tide, people say, *my god, what a stench*,
But to me it was more entrancing than I will
Ever be able to explain; it was sex and death
And time, and every far corner of the planet,

The liquors of all the lives that are and were,
Something ancient beyond any explanations,
Something that had always been there before
Even the uncountable lives that filled it now,
Something bigger than land, the biggest idea
There is that you can touch or be drowned in,
The biggest thing that's real, that's right here,
That we can't dismiss or explain, or lie about.
I never did forget that night. I was frightened
And fascinated in about the same proportions.
In a lot of ways we never did leave the ocean,
Did we, as a species, as shy naked mammals?
It still sloshes around in our innermost rooms.
You know what I mean; you have stood there
Too staring at it for reasons you can't explain.   ·

Gordon Kelly Answers
a Reporter's Question

Early in the summer of 1928 a boy, aged sixteen,
Jumped a San Diego & Imperial Valley Railroad
Freight train to see something of his new country.
He had been born in Moose Jaw in Saskatchewan
But recalled no more than endless shawling snow.
I learned to chisel rides on trains, he said, seventy
Years later, and to cook stew with the bindlestiffs,
And outwit the road bulls, those are the train cops.
And I learned to never argue with a gun. So much
Of what happened I don't have any real words for,
He said. You say *generous*, or *unimaginably poor*,
And they don't catch the guy who shared his meal
Without a word, or folks I met living in the woods,
In huts they made from stones, and chunks of bark.
So after that I go to sea, I got to Hawaii and Brazil,
And then a career in television, made some money
Using the name people know me as, Art Linkletter,
But I never forgot my railroad days. You think our
Country is one place and you discover it's another.
We use big idea words like *economies* and *politics*,
But there's still hungry kids, and huts in the woods.
I don't know how to fix it, but I know we can't lie.
So to answer your question what I remember best?
I guess the man who shared his sandwich with me.
He didn't even hesitate! *That's* who we can still be.

Choosing a Baseball Bat

The second son, having made the school baseball team,
Informs his startled father that they are under-equipped
In the matter of bats—sticks, hammers, the implements
Of destruction, the tool of the trade, the thunder lumber,
As the salesman says cheerfully. There is a dense forest
Of bats against the wall, gleaming graphite and brilliant
Maple, aluminum in every conceivable shade and sheen,
And the father gets absorbed in the names, the Torpedos
And Thunderclubs, Phantoms and Cyclones, the Patriots
And Nitros, Magnums and Maxxums, Rayzrs and Ultras,
And, rivetingly, the Freak, which comes in thirteen sizes,
Which makes you wonder. The father, a terrible baseball
Player as a boy, admires but does not say anything about
The extraordinary lean loveliness of the ash bats hanging
Lonely at the far end. The boy chooses a bright red metal
Hammer, takes a few swings, waggles it a bit, hoists it up
On his shoulder, says *this'll do*, and the sacramental hour
Passes, as all holy moments must. But they do happen, as
Fast and terrifying as a baseball fired right at your noggin.
The batter's job, the second son says, is to identify a pitch
As soon as it leaves a pitcher's hand. Seeing is everything,
He says, and for once we are in complete and utter accord.

Bear

You know how sometimes there's a moment when everyone
In the moment is startled by what happened without warning?
This morning I remember an evening when this happened, at
The Lutheran minister's enormous dark echoing old mansion
Just across the street from the Catholic church and the Jewish
Temple; our main road must have been zoned Major Religion.
I was a Cub Scout, huddled by the fireplace, ready for the test
That would advance us Wolves to Bears. This was a big event
In our lives, don't laugh; it was perhaps the biggest thing ever,
Even bigger than First Confession for us mostly Catholic kids,
Because you had to *earn* Bear, whereas you couldn't get away
From First Confession, during which we admitted to sins we'd
Borrowed from older brothers, often in exchange for cold cash,
Which makes you wonder. Anyway there we were, in uniform,
Ready for the exam, lined up by height by the fire, the minister
Prepared to proctor, our glorious new badges waiting on a desk,
When we realized that one among us was not prepared for Bear.
We stared at each other. I think now we were all quietly hoping
To be saved by somebody else. The reverend led us in the Oath.
But when the questioning began we all deliberately made errors
So as not to advance. The reverend, God rest his soul, could see
That something was up, but he had the wisdom to leave it alone.
A graceful man, as I remember, with a bristling russet mustache.
I suppose our den meeting was over soon after that, bear badges
Sitting untouched on the reverend's desk. I suppose we did earn
Them eventually, and then earn our Arrows of Light, and so on.
The minister's house was eventually sold to a Catholic religious

Order which arose in India from the missionary muscle of Saint Thomas, who fled to the far corners of the earth after examining The Christ. Another quiz by a fire long ago, with quiet epiphany.

Paper Route

Mister Moore, who drank; his oldest son paid the bill without looking at me.
The apartment with the dogs who ate two paperboys, leaving only the shoes.
The Morrows who once paid me with a hundred-dollar bill, keep the change.
The Sunderlands, who wanted the paper unfolded and laid flat under a stone,
Which I did, because Mrs S left candy bars for me in an aluminum milk-box.
The house that left me cash in envelopes nicked from all manner of churches.
The Clearys with the dog who waited for me all afternoon with rising hunger.
Mrs Muller, whose lawn had not been cut for fifty years and had huge snakes.
Mr Harris, the basketball coach, whose son's low rim we tore down, dunking,
And never had the guts to admit it, although he knew, and never again tipped.
The Carrolls, who had a different excuse every week for never paying the bill,
Which when you think about it, is a subtle creative achievement, isn't that so?
The houses where no one was ever home night or day. The house where I saw
A child tied to the doghouse with a plastic clothesline. The houses where men
Shouted at women and children and dogs. The houses where there was a slight
Chance you might see the teenage daughter and her friends sunbathing in back.
The houses with parts of cars and refrigerators and dryers scattered in the yard.
The house where the man always invited you in for a soda but you never went.
The house where the old lady didn't pick up her papers for five days and a cop
Investigated and found her deceased out back by a statue of the Blessed Virgin.
The house where the old lady left me a plate of cookies every blessed Tuesday.
All those newspapers and families and shards of families. For the longest time,
The tale in my family was comical: Remember when Brian had the paper route
And never had the drive to collect more money due than would buy candy bars
But the brother who took over the route from me deftly and smoothly collected
Enough money for a year in college? And I would laugh too, because all it was
Then was a way to get pin money. But now I wonder if I collected more stories

Along those streets than I ever realized, because here I am, all these years later,
Seeing that kid tied to the doghouse as clear as day, his moon face, the brilliant
Rope, the dense knot with which it was tied, a knot no child could ever unravel.

My Second Confession

The first time you go to confession it's mostly Ritual,
For all the hurry and worry and crinkling new clothes;
There's nothing to actually confess at the age of eight,
And the whole event is about admittance and presents:
The first rosary rising from its shining box like a cobra,
Your own Bible bound in supple pliable white calfskin,
Your aunt wondering who murdered the poor wee calf
And if that bloody git had to go to confession too, yeh?
It's the *next* confession that's got hair on it, as my aunt
Was also fond of mumbling. You ask your older sisters
If you can borrow some of their more sophisticated sins,
Something heavier than *I dishonored my mom and dad*,
Everyone uses that one, poor Father behind his wooden
Panel hearing that twenty times a day chirped by babies
Totally unaware of the thousand ways they will later do
Exactly that. You can borrow the sin of self-abuse, says
An older sister which sends all my sisters into hysterics
Before they slam their bedroom door to talk about boys.
And so I ambled into the dense velvet dark of the booth
And knelt, and Father, catching the creak of the kneeler,
Slid the rattling maple panel back behind the iron grille,
And I said Bless me Father for I have sinned previously,
And he made an odd sound in his nose and said Perhaps
You mean grievously, which I most sincerely doubt, and
I warmed him up with dishonoring of mother and father,
And he said something I didn't catch and then I told him
I had beaten up my younger brothers and in my memory

140

He said cheerfully Ah isn't that what kid brothers are for,
And then I went with self-abuse. He made that odd noise
In his nose again but this time it didn't stop. I was afraid
Maybe he was having a Brain Seizure like my aunts said
The Mets players had eleventy times a game every game.
I waited for a while and finally Father came back around.
His voice was a little shaky but he sounded fairly healthy.
I believe I must have a wee priestly chat with your sisters
About leading lambs astray with what seems to be funny,
He said. In the meantime, for your penance I want you to
Enjoy this really lovely day as much as you possibly can,
Will you do that? Yes, Father, I said, and ran off, thrilled.
This confession stuff, it seemed to me, was as easy as pie.

Surfing Jones Beach

One day when I was strong and supple I went surfing
With my brother the day after a roaring thunderstorm.
We stared at the grim mountainous swell twice as big
As anything we had ever seen—and dove in, terrified.
I wasn't brave enough to admit I wasn't brave enough
To enjoy the line between abject fright and utter thrill,
Plus I was pretty much the raggediest surfer in history,
Content to hug the board and try not to be decapitated,
And I surrendered happily after perhaps three minutes,
But my brother stayed in the roiling ocean a long time,
And I think that was the first time I realized how *other*
He was, how alive to another species of joy altogether
Than me—how we could be so close, dressed the same
As children, sleeping in the same room for many years,
Mistaken as twins with our matching bristled crewcuts,
Shoulder to shoulder in a thousand family photographs,
But become men of wildly different clans and passions;
But that is exactly what happened. You can love a man
After you leave the languages only you two ever spoke,
It turns out, and the deep quiet ways I love my brothers
And they love me have been gifts beyond measurement
And beyond any expectation, too, a sea of wild currents.
When he finally came in he was smiling and speechless,
I remember that. Not the first time silence was eloquent.

Dechi Palmo

Discovered a few moments ago that my sister, my sole sister,
The sister I have admired for more than fifty years, the sister
Who rocked my cradle with her toe as she did her homework,
The sister who was never especially leery of punching us out
When she felt we deserved it which I have to say yes we did,
This sister has a name I never ever heard before this morning.
Dechi Palmo she is called in the Tibetan Buddhist monastery
She graces. *Depa for short*, she says cheerfully, on the phone.
I know where that phone is, the only one in all the monastery.
It's hanging on the wall outside the kitchen where she works,
When she is not teaching, or praying, or meditating, or every
One of the thousand other tasks she does silently and smiling.
It means Happiness Glorious Woman, she says, or Happiness
Glorious She Who Meditates. I nearly faint with seething joy.
Sometimes, not all that often, but more than we maybe admit,
Things line up exactly right, all hilarious and wild and bright,
And you see a thing just as it really is, deep in its holy bones.
You think that's never going to happen again but then it does.
You can't command it, you can't make it stay, you cannot do
Much of anything except slouch there grinning and mystified,
It turns out, but to be occasionally grinning and mystified, ah!

Father Man

In a coffee shop one morning in Provo, Utah, as I am reading the hoop news,
A very small child, perhaps age three, appears suddenly and says Father Man,
Could you reach me the jellies? And can I have two waffles? And a lot butter?
And for a moment, not even a moment, it was like thirteen seconds, she is my
Daughter, in all sorts of bewildering and shivering ways. Her utter confidence
In me, her eyes the color of winter just like my daughter who is now a woman,
Her making a serious run at as much sugar as she can mow through before her
Mother blows the whistle—even the way she appeared magically at my elbow
With a run of questions like salmon running rapids. She could tell I was a dad
Somehow—the best compliment ever. We stare at each other, plotting butter.

Revelation

I am soaking in Revelation, in the King James, just before dawn,
The dog snoring in his chair, everyone in the house sick and abed.
Perhaps this is a dangerous idea, reading Revelation before sunrise.
Perhaps I should absorb Revelation with a seat belt and a whiskey.
But there are cracks in the wild lines, through which roaring music
Pours in: *this saith he that holdeth the seven stars in his right hand,*
I know thy works, and thy labour, and thy patience. These children,
Then, the angry one, the wheezing one, the one flying up and away,
You'll keep them in your hand, the hand with the stars? You swear?
Remember therefore from whence thou art fallen and repent and do
The first works; or else I will come unto thee quickly, and remove . . .
No no—no need. I am on task: patience, dishes, laundry, insurance.
I read the fine print on the refinance. *I know thy poverties, but thou*
Art rich, and well I know that too, my old friend, well I know these
Tumultuous gifts, the woman with the cascading hair, I witness her,
The daughter here for seven seconds before rushing back to college,
I witness her, the sons battling to stay civil as they thrash to be men,
I witness them; I used to be them. *He that hath an ear, let him hear.*
You could take me back in your right hand this instant, and I would
Go laughing, yes I would. The immeasurable gift of loud high chaos.
I know thy works and charity and service and faith, and thy patience.
Yes. You dwelleth in them, the four of them moaning sick. Your eye
Is on the dog, the moist disgruntle of sparrows in the sheening dawn,
The heron like a paleozoic archangel against the sway and surf of fir.
I will give a new name written, which no man knoweth, save he who
Receiveth it, but I do know it and sing it, a name with the four words
Used for the gifts who are sleeping. *He that hath an ear, let him hear.*

His Empty Hand

Or here's a story. A man just back from elsewhere tells it to me.
The place I was, he says, the law was that a thief lost his fingers,
The theory being that he could not steal again, but an accusation
Was the same as conviction. A man I knew, his son stole bottles
Of water for a friend who had a new child and basically no cash.
The son is sentenced to lose his left hand, but the dad intercedes,
Offering his hand for his son's. His offer is accepted by the cops,
An officer comes with an axe, they bury the hand with ceremony
Out back. Now, when this father, who was a friend of mine, tells
Me this story, and sure I gaped at his empty hand, I kept thinking
What's the meaning of this, you know? What's the message here,
Other than savagery and what, if you were polite, you would call
Cultural disparity, you know? And it is the dad who answers this.
Why, wouldn't you give both hands for your sons and daughters?
He asks. Wouldn't you give anything, if they are in some trouble?
In a way I feel shame, he says, because what happened is so clear,
As if I am boasting of my love for my son. But all mothers would
Do this, and all fathers. If you would not then you are not a parent,
You are only a means through which your child entered the world.
To only be a gate, not a man willing to lose himself, that is shame.
Is that not the essence of your believing in the Father and the Son?

The Order of Melchizedek

Bizarrely enough, a priest friend of mine says,
What I remember clearest from my ordination
Is that when we were all sprawled on the floor
Face-first and silent and awed before the One,
My nose was freezing. I think every single guy
Felt the same way. There we were, soon to join
The Order of Melchizedek, priests of The Lord
Until we breathed our last on this lovely planet,
And we are all thinking *Lord, hurry the bishop!*
I mean, you have to laugh. I have often thought
In these years here at the end of my priesthood,
How exactly right and holy and human the start
Was, though, as a priest. Everyone was suitably
Awed by the vow, and the ritual, and the smoke
And ancient tradition of it; it's very real, and he
Who would make fun of it is missing the power
And glory of the promise—we were mere boys,
Taking a really unimaginable leap into wild lives,
Not knowing anything, really, of long loneliness,
Or how you can be given a sort of clan and tribe,
As a priest, of friends and parishioners, and kids
You baptize—I think I have twenty godchildren.
But my point is how very human the first minute
Is, sprawled out on the floor, not thinking of awe
Or prayers or promises, but of your ice-cold nose.
That's the exact right honest human way to begin.

Learning to Shoot

I was maybe nine years old and my brother was seventeen.
As I remember he was lanky and surly and totally my hero.
There's no reason for him showing me how to cup the ball
Properly on your hand, your wrist cocked, your other hand
Only the gentlest of guides as you get the ball up and away
With backspin—no, you got to *snap* the wrist like that, see,
So the ball spins, that gives you a soft shot that will bounce
Around the rim and fall in often as not. He wasn't much for
Hoop, my brother, not then, and I remember it was freezing,
And the rim was sagging, and the ball was as heavy as mud,
But we stayed there shooting forever. Why he was so gentle
With me as the evening grew darker and colder is a mystery.
We don't remember much of what we're sure we remember,
That's a fact, and a remarkably awkward fact it can become,
But I am not sure we are as delighted that we remember just
Scraps and shards and flashes and shivers of what happened
As much as we should be. Maybe he was always kind to me,
And I don't remember that, or maybe he had just battled our
Dad and felt stupid and went out to cool off, and there I was,
Struggling with the ball. Maybe just the fact that I remember
Anything whatsoever of that icy muddy moment is a miracle.
We all have the itch to draw conclusions, to discern patterns,
And it's fun to think that this was the seed of my hoop jones,
That my brother's hand on my hand, showing me what to do,
Was the beginning of a game that changed and defined a life,
But I am beginning to get it, finally, that a story can stand up
Alone, that a story means itself, it doesn't really carry freight.

We load stories with meaning, and they have muscular backs,
But when you leave them alone they are stunningly articulate,
It turns out. So here—here are two brothers, learning to shoot,
As the afternoon dies, on a winter day. They are always there.

1945

Here is my dad in Manila. He is twenty-three years old.
He is a master sergeant. His task is to read photographs
And maps and charts and interviews with local planters
And residents in areas which the armies of the Alliance
Wish to liberate from the armies of the empire of Japan.
He works in the main building of Santa Ana Race Track
And lives in a tent nearby. It is roaring hot. He is lonely.
He was married a year ago; their honeymoon was a day.
He is sure he is going to die in the forthcoming invasion.
His task is to inform invaders about danger both natural,
Like swift tide changes and hidden reefs, and unnatural,
Like mines and ammunition depots and gun placements.
In August an Army Air Corps pilot brings him the films
From reconnaissance flights over Hiroshima. My father
Examines the film closely and tells the pilot it's an error,
The film is blank, there's zip where the city is supposed
To be. Yes sir, says the pilot. Maybe you are not hearing
Me here, corporal, says my dad. This is useless; the film
Is empty. That is what we photographed over Hiroshima,
Sir, says the Air Corps man. I am sure we were on target,
Sir. Positive. My dad, disgruntled, pores over the photos
Again, and slowly, he says, years later, I realized he was
Correct, and that the films were accurate, and Hiroshima
Was . . . obliterated. Our dad has always chosen his words
Carefully and he uses the word *obliterated* when he talks
About that moment in the ancient bloody story of people.
Another man might have made some hay from the detail

That he was the first man in history to see nothing where
Hiroshima used to be, but not our dad. Our dad says that
Was a horrifying tragedy and it saved a million lives. He
Says it was a terrible thing that should never occur again.
He says he sat there and realized that probably the battle
Was over and he could go home and thousands of people
Were roasted and a million more twisted for a generation.
He says no one can count the people saved by the bombs
And no one can justify the horror of them either. He says
Anyone who thinks he has something smart to say here is
A smug fool. He says this sitting at the kitchen table next
To the girl who waited for him to come back even though
They were both sure he would die in the invasion. Two or
Three times a day, if you look carefully, you can see them
Holding hands. It's like some young part of them can't get
Over the fact that he made it home. So many others didn't.

Poem for Grace Farrell (1976–2011)

A thin column in the newspaper; she died in an alcove
Outside Saint Brigid's Church. She was from Wicklow.
She had been an artist. She came here at age seventeen.
She drank. She married a man who slept on the avenue,
Not near the church. He didn't like the church and said
That the church talked to him at night in a stern rumble.
He beat her. Her friends on the street beat him and told
Him to stay away from her. Her alcove had a roof on it,
In a sense, as there was a construction scaffold above it.
The folks like us—nobody knows us until we are dead,
Said a friend of hers on the street. Her family in Ireland
Accepted her body, from the medical examiner's office.
We told them that she was homeless, but they chose not
To believe that, said the examiner. Her name was Grace.
So that's the end of the article. But what if that's not the
End at all? What if the old church spoke to Grace Farrell
That night, held her in its southern arm, sang very gently
To her as she died, caught her spirit as it hit the scaffold,
And handed it up, weeping for the sweet broken woman?
Couldn't that be? Couldn't it be that we don't know who
She was and wanted to be, and maybe she was a wonder?
That could be. Maybe she was what she was invited to be.
Maybe her soul said yes to pain in this world to save kids
Somewhere else. Maybe she was brave in ways we never
Will know now. Every time I think I know something for
Sure I get the gift of not being sure at all; isn't that grace?

The Cross

Probably an olive or acacia, as far as scholars can determine.
Of course there are scholars who have poked into the matter.
The Roman Empire sensibly used the most accessible wood.
Me personally I would bet on the acacia which grows bigger
And broader and quicker than olive. You wonder if someone
Grew them for just this use. A market niche with an imperial
Budget, who could argue with that as a business model? Not
To mention the excellent public relations aspects of assisting
The mills of justice, the civic equilibrium, the battles against
Criminals and radicals. Imagine it: an acacia grows in Judea,
Let's say in Ashkelon, near the sea. It is harvested at twenty,
Planed with its brothers, and trundled to Jerusalem. The load
Is stamped and recorded, bills of sale and receipts are issued,
A few of the timbers are mysteriously lost in transit and filed
As cost of business, and one ends up on Golgotha—the Skull.
Poor creature, remembered only for its last burden. But recall
The birds it housed, the birds it sensed whizzing past—*deror*,
The swallows and swifts, the small gleaming knives in flight,
And *selaw*, the quail in their vast flocks, carpeting the acacias
In October like feathery jackets, and *anafas*, the patient heron,
And *hasidah* the stork and *larus* the gull and *nesher* the eagle,
And certainly *yonah*, the dove. Imagine our acacia held seven
Dove nests in its twenty years. Imagine the gentle burbling of
Chicks is the last music it remembered as the axe bit. Imagine
It never knew or imagined the gaunt being it held at the finish.
Poor thing, remembered for what it never knew it was bent to;
But celebrated quietly this morning, as another young life lost.

153

The Actual You

What are the things I should know about being homeless
That I would never imagine myself? I ask a girl who was
Homeless from age thirteen to age seventeen. You never
Saw a nicer more pleasant neatly dressed kid in your life,
This kid. The only way you can tell who she used to be is
That she has a bunch of steel teeth. Any hint of difficulty,
She says, you move. Move anyways, on general principle.
Any safe spot you find will eventually be found by others.
As for new friends, trust but verify, as some old president
Said. Learn to lie with a totally straight face. Brush teeth!
I still have trouble not lying immediately and defensively.
That's a problem for me. I got so good at it that it's tough
To not be good at it anymore. The best way to get by is to
Perform, to not be who you really are, so the actual you is
Not in danger. You can shuck the person you perform like
A snake shucks a skin. Teachers here tell me I ought to be
In theater, I should try out for plays and musicals, but that
Is exactly what I am trying not to be, which is good at not
Being the real me anymore. Does this make sense? *You'd
Be a natural*, my teachers say, and I have to laugh because
Natural at not being me is who I don't want to be anymore.

The Whole Weasel Question

Consider the case of a mathematician, in this case
My oldest brother, who is (a) halved by an illness,
(b) stilled completely by it, and (c) reduced to ash.
Trust me, he would be the first to note that finally
He finished his travels at 0.00416666667 of what
He weighed for a long time. I bet then he'd spend
Weeks poking into what else weighed exactly that.
I'd get a terse note with a list in his meticulous ink:
The cardinal on average weighs 0.992 of a pound,
And the long-tailed weasel weighs exactly a pound.
A letter like that is exactly like a zen koan, I think.
It's as much a door as a statement. Let us consider
That we have all just now received this terse letter.
It sits there grinning on the table next to the coffee.
I don't know about you, but *I* am going to dive into
The whole weasel question. We have so little time,
And there's so much to be discovered. I want to be
Able to be conversant about this the next time I see
My brother. He'll want to know. He'll have missed
A *lot* of time that could have been devoted to these
Things, and *someone* has to carry the ball, whether
It's weasels or cardinals or cancer. How mortifying
It will be if he asks me about something, and I have
To say *I didn't pay attention, man*, and he will stare
At me with that laser stare and not even have to say,
And what was it you did instead of paying attention?

Mrs. Job

There was a man in the land of Uz, whose name was Job;
And he was essentially a blameless dude, and unarrogant,
And he was blessed with seven sons, and three daughters,
Which is a lot of children, and where, I ask politely, is the
Part of the Book of Job where we talk about Job's spouse,
Who is conspicuously not discussed in the back and forth
With his buddies and then suddenly the Big Guy Himself
Answering out of the whirlwind and commanding old Job
To gird up his loins, which loins were undeniably vigorous
Previous to the Lord interrupting Job, and after the Maker
Finishes one of the greatest eloquent scoldings of all time,
He grants old Job another seven sons and three daughters,
Again without the slightest thanks for the astounding Mrs.
Job who suddenly has twenty count them twenty children
With no mention of her humor, or the vast hills of diapers,
Or her wit which survived kids throwing up and the sheep
Wandering off, and plagues of locusts and things like that.
A good editor, I feel, would have asked for just a glancing
Nod to the wry hero of the tale, at least acknowledgment;
Something like a new last line after *So Job died, being old
and full of days*, which might read, And also passed a most
Amazing woman, of whom nothing other than the blessing
Was ever said, her heart being a gift beyond calculation by
Man, her mind sharp, her tongue gentle, her hands a mercy,
And her very presence full reason to kneel in prayer at that
Which the Lord in His mercy has made and granted briefly.
A line like that would only hint at her, but it's a start, right?

Psalm 46.5, in Which They Come for the Body

They are coming for the body; a nurse certifies
That who she was is no longer resident in what
She was, selah. *They* turn out to be one woman.
Her name is Helene. Selah. She eases what was
A woman onto a gurney. A daughter assists her.
Though the waters roar and be troubled, we will
Not fear, though the mountains vanish in the sea.
Selah. Would you like your mother to be facing
Up or down? Up, please, selah. She zips the bag.
She did believe, yes she did, selah, she received
The glories of the Lord each and every day with
Her eyes which remained hawkish until her final
Breath. Is that so? says Helene, selah. Transplant
Candidates, then, certainly. Sign here . . . and here.
I will drive very carefully, absolutely. His mercy
Upon her soul, selah. She trusted in thee. Refuge
She will discover in thee, and her husband's arm,
And her mother's kiss, and all calamities are past,
Selah, and housekeeping will come for the sheets.
God is in the midst of her, and God shall help her.
There is a river; the waters of which have no end;
Amen and then again amen. In the lobby a father
Is reading the sports section while his child gulps
The biggest soda I have ever seen on this blessed
Wild and weary earth; amen and then again amen.

A Shimmer of Something

Well, the aged mother of the woman who married me died,
And there are so many stories both sad and hilarious to tell,
But let me tell you just one, because it is little and not little.
At her Mass, after the miracle, but before the electric bread
Went into every soul, as people are shuffling slowly toward
The altar, everyone in the line on the left side, as they came
To the front pew, touched my wife. Some bent down to hug
Her. Some touched her hair gently. Some just placed a hand
On her shoulder. One woman reached down and cupped her
Face in her hands for an instant. Sure I wept. We touch each
Other when we have no other way to speak. We speak many
Languages without words. We are so much wilder and wiser
Than we know. There are so very many of us without words,
Speaking the most amazing and eloquent languages; we sing
With our hands. I have seen it happen. You have seen it, too.
It's a little thing, but there's a shimmer of something beyond
Vast. See, I am trying to say an epic thing in this small poem,
And here we are at the end of the poem, where I stop talking.

A Small Poem

To say thanks for reading this poem,
And all the other ones I've inflicted
Upon you over all these years. I *did*
Think, many times, of your gracious
Acceptance of that which you didn't
Ask for, and perhaps did not actually
Want; but I never said thanks, did I?
So I do. I wanted to . . . I don't know,
Connect, somehow, though we don't
Know each other; maybe that is why
I so wanted to connect, so often with
Just a little poem, like this. It matters
To connect, in some sweet holy way,
More than we can gauge. My sincere
Thanks for the gift of your attention;
Witness is our great work. *You* knew
That, I know—I'm just reminding us.

Maybe the Future Is a Story That Hates to Wait

Me, personally, I think stories are starving to be told.
I think there are millions there, jostling and elbowing
To get to the parachute bay and snatching any chance
Whatsoever, no matter how remote, to get themselves
Told at last, or retold—the latter meaning born again,
Really. Consider the immortality implications of *that*.
Maybe stories are like kids who are ideas before flesh.
Maybe kids are ideas who get laboriously fleshed out,
Like novels. Maybe children are made of stories more
Than they are of bone and hair and turkey sandwiches.
Maybe the way to think of a teenager is as a wry story
That's all verb and no object as yet. Maybe we guzzle
Forty stories with every breath we draw and they soak
Into us and flavor and thicken and spice the wild stew
We are. Maybe we are all the stories we ever told and
Will tell when they let us see their gleaming first lines.
Maybe the future means a vast story that hates to wait.
Maybe we are made of more stories we forgot than of
Stories we think to remember. Maybe what we forget
Are stories that realize they were in the wrong mouth.
Maybe every story has to find the right teller. Maybe I
Had to wait all this time to be able to tell you this story.

At Our Lady of Unanswerable Questions School

Another headlong visit to another burbling seething sea of shaggy miracles.
I wear my good black shirt so as to indicate respect and some small dignity.
We are supposed to talk about writing but as usual things spin away utterly,
And we are arguing about basketball and religion and if Montana is heaven.
I say Montana cannot possibly be heaven because it's snowed for two years
Straight there, grizzlies have learned to ski, has no one read the newspaper?
Then a round kid in back raises his hand. He sort of sneaks it up quietly,
As if he wants to ask a question but he's not actually sure he should. Yessir,
I say, how can I help you? When babies are aborted, he says, is there a birth
Certificate? You can't get a birth certificate if no one ever gave you a name,
Right? And if you are going to get aborted, no one would want to name you.
But if you don't get a name or a birth certificate were you actually a person?
His hand has stayed shyly in the air as he asked his three questions, I notice;
As if as long as his hand was an antenna no one could interrupt him or tease
Him or say his questions were stupid or inappropriate or this is not the place
Nor the time for such questions. But when is the time for questions like his?

The Flying Eagle Patrol

In the high summer of my thirteenth year on this lovely planet
I was mailed to Boy Scout summer camp in a sprawling forest
For a life term, though I guess it was really only fourteen days.
I was muddled at woodcraft as I was at everything else then,
And finished very nearly last in tracking, swimming, canoeing,
Archery, and orienteering, this last an utter conundrum for me;
I recall my patrolmates finally gently taking away my compass
And asking me to just sit quietly until they would lead me back
To our camp, my spectacles knocked awry by jeering branches.
I remember when we got our orienteering assignment someone
Would lead me to a little open knoll in the rippling sea of pines
And oaks and maples and I would sit there happily in the broad
Sun for hours, I guess, watching for birds and speculating about
Lunch. I wonder now that the Flying Eagle Patrol was so gentle
To me, its most useless member, and these were the years when
Boys are cruel to each other, for fear of being least and weakest;
But they *were* kind, and I remember their totally genuine delight
When I earned my single merit badge, for making both a roaring
Fire and a stew. I remember their faces, around that startling fire,
How they laughed—not at me for having finally done something
Well, but at the surprise of it; the gift of unexpectedness, perhaps.
Or maybe they were smiling at my probably hair-raising stew; but
They ate every scrap of it, and the one among us who was best in
The woods was the Eagle who quietly washed the pots and plates.
Perhaps, all these years later, I should remember my helplessness,
And either chew my liver or try to smile ruefully, but it's the pots
Clean as a whistle that I remember, and the whistling of the Eagle
Coming to retrieve me from my knoll high above the seas of trees.

Something That Sees Them All

A man is stopped at a traffic light, one of those lights that stays red for a week,
But he knows this, and is cool with it, because it happens every day, so usually
He fiddles with the radio, or ponders what to make for supper, but this time he
Happens to see a terrifying tiny war in the adjacent hedges—a sharpshin hawk
Is after the chicks in a scrub jay nest, and the jays are totally losing their minds.
The hawk is hopping around in the hedge trying to get a good angle for the kill
And the jays are playing wild shrieking defense. As far as I can tell, they are in
A tight zone, with one guarding the nest and the other jumping out at the hawk.
You wouldn't believe how loud this all is but no one else seems to hear a thing.
The jay in the front of the zone feints and stabs at the hawk but I suspect he has
To be careful not to get too close or he or she will be the meat. The hawk holds
On a branch for two seconds; the jays stay in their zone; the light turns; and the
Hawk sails off. I have to focus on driving and I cannot see if there is disgruntle,
Or delight, or relief, or fury, or a quick chat about who should have been where
On defense. In my mirror for an instant I see the hawk, rising; perhaps the most
Beautiful of birds, big enough to capture what it wants and small enough to zip
Through trees and hedges like a russet dagger; and then it is gone and the battle
Is a memory and there are so many intense stories like this, it boggles the mind.
Perhaps what we really mean when we say God is Something that sees them all.

Your Dad

An eighth-grade class has asked me to talk about being afraid of stuff.
We didn't set out in this direction but the talk turned honest suddenly
And here we are. You can't lie to kids like this nor can you issue crap.
You have to answer them straight up and hope for the best. I'm scared
About my kids, I say. That scares me most of all. They'll get hurt, and
I can't save them. *Your* dad worries about that too, you know, at night,
When you're asleep. He stands by your bed and thinks he's not a good
Enough dad for you. Believe me he does this. He'll never admit it, you
Know, but he does it. Trust me. I know. We worry you won't get to be
The coolest greatest you ever for some reason—a truck hits you, a bad
Marriage, drugs. Sure we are scared. You think all dads are stern guys,
Always on your case about homework, always saying the wrong thing,
Always lecturing about how the price of independence is responsibility,
But you don't see us by your bed at night, terrified. Nor do your moms.
We say we are going up to check that the kids are asleep, to turn down
The heat, to dim the light, and we do these things, but then we all stand
There, scared. Some of us cry and some pray and some do both at once.
Some guys bend down and tuck their kids in but most of us try to get it
Together again before we go downstairs and say I think they are asleep,
But they are devious animals, those children of yours, and who knows?

Poem on the Essential Impossibility
of Writing a Decent Poem in Gaelic

Because whenever I try to say something in a second language,
Even a second language I can barely grasp though I have loved
It since I was a tiny boy swimming in it like a man in a brilliant
Strange sea all alluring and murky and frightening and swirling,
The language you want to enter looks at you puzzled and agape
At what you are trying to get it to do. I think you all know what
I mean here. The language is much older than you are and bears
Itself with a dignity and heft that has seen empires come and go,
Whereas the average badger is smarter than me and can prove it.
You cannot ask a second language to dance. You must approach
It hat in hand, as it were, and negotiate, see if there is a common
Place to stand for a moment, singing. I spill my words on a table
And the ancient language stares at them for a while, with a smile.
I think you all know what I mean here. Sometimes what happens
Then is that the old language slides away from the table and that
Is the end of that, but sometimes it takes my words and makes of
Them something with music in it—a poem that's not all that bad.

Dán faoin dodhéantacht bhunúsach a bhaineann le dán cuibheasach maith a scríobh sa Ghaeilge

Mar aon uair a bhainim triail as rud a rá i dteanga eile
fiú dara theanga nach bfuil agam uirthi ach leath eolas
cé go raibh grá agam di ó na laethanta a bhíos i mo bhuachaillín ag snámh inti
mar fear i bhfarraige lonrach, ilmheallacach, modartha, scanrúil, guairneach.
Féachann sí ort, an teanga a mbíonn fonn ortsa dul isteach inti, féachann sí ort
go béaloscailte, faoi dhubhiontas ar a bhfuil tú ag iarraidh a dhéanamh.
Tá 'fhios ag cách faoi seo. Tá an teanga i bhfad níos sine ná tusa.
Iompraíonn sí í féin go huasal, go daingean, teacht agus imeacht gach impireachta feicthe
aici. Muise, tá an gnáthbhroc féin níos glice ná mise, 's is féidir leis é a chruthú.
Ní féidir leat cuireadh damhsa a thabhairt do dara theanga. Caithfidh tú teacht ina láthair
go humhal, socrú a dhéanamh léi, féachaint an bhfuil comháit ann chun seasamh seal, ag
canadh. Doirtím mo chuid focal ar bord agus stánann an tseantheanga orthu tamaill,
's í ag miongháire. Tá 'fhios ag cách faoi seo.
Uaireanta, 's é a tharlaíonn ná go sleamhnaíonn an tseantheanga ón mbord agus sin sin.
Ach anois is arís tógann sí mo chuid focal agus déanann sí díobh áit a bhfuil ceol inti
    dán nach féidir le h-éinne mórán a rá ina choinne.

translated by Ger Killeen

166

Mr. Stengel

Well, here's today's tiny story that isn't tiny:
Once there was a legendary baseball manager
Famous for cheerfully mangling the language
And being cruel to some players and offering
Whopping lies to newspaper reporters, just to
Annoy them, but this was also true of him; he
Would quietly spend any amount of time with
Blind fans, especially children, as long as they
Wanted, and they could gently run their hands
Giggling over his face, as long as they wanted.
That's all. That's all I wanted to tell you today.
Just that. An old man offering his face to a kid.

Four

A child dies on Independence Day, in the evening,
Just after she watches *101 Dalmatians* for the 101st
Time, probably, says her father. I hated that movie
With a powerful hate after the eightieth time or so,
You couldn't help hating it, I wanted to just shriek
When she put it on again, but that day we huddled
In the bed, and it was the greatest movie there ever
Was. She was laughing fit to bust at the funny part.
She was four. There is nothing more amazing I can
Ever say than she was laughing fit to bust. One day
A kid who knew full well she was going to die that
Night huddled in bed with her parents and laughed
Fit to bust. You remember that when you need that.
I will too. We'll shake on it. She went out laughing.
You remember that. I will too. That will be praying.

Kestrel

A name is a sound. A name is a written or vocalized marker or label
For things that are complex. We use names as terse codes, primarily
To save time in reference or conversation. Names are not the things.
We know this but we forget. A sparrowhawk, for example, is a verb
Of incredibly complicated proportions. As is a huckleberry bush, an
Essayist, your teacher, god. The marker *god* is from a Hebrew word
Meaning to invade or overcome. No one owns the word or the labels
We variously use for the ideas we variously like, detest, or flee from,
Or all of the above, depending on the week, and who is sick or dead.
We know this but we forget. We begin to think names have meaning.
They have no meaning. They have no weight. They are not the thing.
No matter how loud you shout the name it does not indicate wisdom
Or possession or ownership or insight or a preferred customer status.
Names can be lyrical and loaded with ancient aura and amazing tales
But they remain labels, markers, sweet sounds we use for shorthand;
We know this but we forget. So it is that every time I think I am sure
About anything having to do with the idea, the blind energetic breath
For which we use the word God, I remind myself to go find a kestrel,
And watch it for a while, and remember that while I *can* say it caught
A mouse, or that it teetered for a remarkable seven minutes on a wire
In the wind without ever being blown over into a hilarious spin cycle,
Or that it holds in the air against the wind like nothing else I ever saw,
I cannot say that I know kestrelness in any but the smallest ways. We
Know this but we forget. Maybe the best way to pray is with your eye.

169

Habemus Ferus Novi Praesulis
(We Have a Wild New Pope)

Would you be pope if you got elected, dad? asks son two
At the tumultuous dinner table, and while once again old
Boring dad launches into a boring disquisition about how
Those men in dresses actually can elect anyone, we don't
Have to have a cardinal or a bishop or even a priest if you
Read the application form carefully, another part of me is
Thinking o no man those little red slippers are not going to
Work for me, and another deeper part is thinking noo *way*,
I really and truly love the woman who married me and I'd
Miss curling up in bed and laughing and those icy feet you
Just have to accept if you are the lucky guy she said yes to,
But then a surprisingly deep door inside opens, and I think,
Man, yeah, I would be pope, if the phone rang, late at night,
Collect call from the Vatican. Oh yes—if I could do it right.
I'd call a meeting of the Curia and say boys, we are letting
Women run everything for the next five years. Each of you
Gets a new boss in high heels. Also we are selling all castle
Properties in toto. From now on we all live in aged convents.
We'll keep the museum properties. No more cars and planes.
We walk and ride bikes. We are going to do what we say we
Want to do—feed the hungry, house the homeless, clothe the
Naked. That's about it. Also people get to elect their bishops,
Like in the old days. Also you can only be pope for ten years.
Mandatory term limits is not such a bad idea. Also rapists get
Sent to jail, like in the real world. Also we will have a trustee
Board made up of nuns and mothers of kindergarten children.

Also we will be joining up again with our Protestant brothers,
Like in the old days before Martin Luther was right. Anyone
Have questions? I need you to help me do what we said we're
All about but a lot of the time we weren't. We can either be an
Insurance company hoarding its cash and power, or we can be
A verb of an idea that changes the world. We can try like crazy
Or we can slowly go out of business. You guys with me or not?

Holding Hands

One time I spent a whole day looking for people holding hands.
It turned out to be one of the most amazing days there ever was.
Right off the bat I saw lots of teens and twenties holding hands,
Couples of every sort and stripe, but I had expected to see that,
As holding hands at that age is really a way of public speaking,
You know what I mean, so what began to knock me out all day
Was everyone else, the three tiny schoolchildren holding hands
As they all waited for the bus, a young man leading an old man
Who was maybe his father, two women who were maybe eighty
Holding hands as they gingerly inched down the museum stairs,
A guy holding out his hand to another guy as the second guy got
Out of a cab that was perched over a gulley filled with rainwater,
A dancer in a poster holding her hands out to two other dancers,
A dad walking along the street with a tiny girl holding his pinky
And the dad half bent down as he walked listening to her talking,
Two girls walking along holding hands until they split by a lamp
Post and then reached for each other again which was cool to see,
A man and a woman coming out of a movie theater and reaching
For each other without looking, that was either cool or they took
Each other for granted, I don't know, but the sight that nailed me
Good and finished off the day and stays with me still weeks later
Was a boy maybe twelve years old or so with a boy maybe nine,
I figured they were brothers coming from school with backpacks
Bouncing as they ran past, the older boy in the lead but his hand
Trailing out behind him like a lifeline for the gasping kid brother,
That was so cool it made me laugh, partly because you could see
That the older brother was hip to the fact that they were seriously

Going to be late unless they ran like hell but no way was he about
To leave his dopey kid brother behind no matter what, but it was
The younger brother's face that I can see right now, a wild sweet
Face with just about everything in it, laughter at how fast they ran
And worry that they were going to be late and mom would be mad
And arrowed intent to keep up with his brother and maybe you will
Say I am dreaming or thinking wishful or whatever but I swear he
Had a glint of mad love for his brother in his face, a kind of shining
Thing, some kind of absolute joy just that they were holding hands.
Well, they rocketed by so fast that they were gone before I could get
Turned around to see if they made the bus or not but that glint, man,
That stays with me. That kid was thrilled to have a hand in his hand,
And really, when you think about it, what could be cooler than that?

Lines on the Tiny Ubiquitous Tattoo That Every Young Woman These Days Appears to Have on Her Lower Spine

Not that I am looking or anything, but there it is,
Time and time and time again, and I find myself
Wondering did they all go to the same tattoo guy
Or what? and when was the meeting at which all
Young ladies in America decided to get tattooed?
And while we are on this subject why are young
Women not as beautiful as women at fifty or so?
How can a young woman be essentially a perfect
And extraordinary example of female beauty but
Somehow it's the woman age fifty with that look
In her eye that nails you to the floor, why is that?
I mean, all the explanations we could summon up
Would be variations on seasoning and experience
And grace under duress and courage against pain
And how facing a lot of things makes you deeper
And cooler and braver and more merciful and so,
Somehow, in ways that I do not understand a bit,
Your average older woman, and of course I have
One particular example in mind, is wild stunning
Beautiful, her waters deeper, her soul hammered
Into a kind of sword that is just riveting to watch.
You almost wish there was a secret mark or sign
That older women would tattoo on their eyelids
As a sign of turbulent and enticing waters ahead,
But I suppose one of the coolest and most lovely

Things about older women is that there's no map
To them, no wisdom that applies, you are utterly
On your own on their wild water. All best wishes!

Poem for Mister Carlos Arredondo, of Boston

One of the quiet things that happens to you when you are a writer,
Or purport to be, or are considered to be, even though all you ever
Did was just keep typing, is that when something sad or terrifying
Happens, people say, *Are you going to write about it?* And mostly
The answer is no, because you have no wisdom, you have nothing
Incisive or wry or wise to say—you are just a guy who types a lot.
And I haven't the slightest urge to add to the ocean of bloody rage
Or vengeful prose or religious muck. But after three of my friends
Were roasted to ash on September 11, I couldn't stop typing about
The men who ran *up* the stairs to help, and after Newtown I could
Not stop writing about the two women who dove *at* the murderer,
And now after Boston I can't stop seeing the runners who ran right
By the finish line to the hospital to give blood, and the people who
Raced toward the blast, and the man whose son died in Najaf, Iraq.
Let me tell you about this man. His son was a Marine corporal. He
Was twenty years old, this kid. After he died his dad drove around
America with a coffin filled with his son's favorite stuff: his soccer
Ball, his battle boots, his dog tags, his church shoes, his teddy bear.
His dad says wars are stupid and we don't fight against war enough.
He moved to Boston, to be near his son's grave. Every year he goes
To the marathon to help out with first aid. When the bomb blew, he
Ran toward the blast and saved a guy. He is who we are at our best.
Murder is an old tired story. It converts and convinces no one. Why
Murderers are so eternally stupid is a puzzle to me. There's always
Women diving at the murderer, and guys running right at the blasts.
Do murderers not pay any attention? Hey, you kids plotting the next
Bomb, do you think people will pay more attention to whatever your

176

Ostensible reason is, if you tear their son to shreds with flying nails?
You think people will stop and say *hey maybe those murderers have
A point?* You stupid thugs: Every nail you fire is a nail in the coffin
Of the thing you claim to love, the thing you claim is holy, the thing
You just damaged and maybe even ruined. Do you guys not pay any
Attention to history? Here's your lesson for today: Osama bin Laden
Wanted to elevate the faith he claimed to love, more than anyone for
A thousand years since it began—but he caused it more damage than
Anyone in a thousand years. His whole life was a joke and a criminal
Attack not only on innocents but on the religion he claimed he loved.
Do you guys not get it? What, you still want to do something savage?
I got an idea: set yourselves on fire. Take your time. We'll consider it
A brave sacrifice. We'll consider that the right victims died, for once.

Poem for a Dear Friend

I don't tell you how much it matters to me that you are my friend.
I'll never tell you, bluntly and face to face. I can't summon words
That way. They only come to my fingers occasionally if I'm silent
And just quit thinking. Our fingers are a lot smarter than we know.
Like today when my fingers want to say something like: your gifts
To me have been ears and humor. We speak some strange language
That few other people speak. I don't know why that's so. It's surely
An accident. It's not like we set out to find each other in the tumult
Of this sweet wilderness. But we did somehow. You can put names
On the finding if you want. The names all mean the same thing. An
Old name is Providence, which is another way to say God, which is
A way to say We Have No Idea How, But We Are Aware of Grace.
There are more names for God than we'll ever know, and one is you.

CPSIA information can be obtained
at www.ICGtesting.com
Printed in the USA
BVHW090214091222
653833BV00010B/546

9 780814 637142